The Genesis of Desire

STUDIES IN VIOLENCE, MIMESIS, AND CULTURE SERIES

The Genesis
of Desire

Jean-Michel Oughourlian

Translated by Eugene Webb

Michigan State University Press · *East Lansing*

⊖ The paper used in this publication meets the minimum requirements of ANSI/
NISO Z39.48-1992 (R 1997) (Permanence of Paper).

 Michigan State University Press
East Lansing, Michigan 48823-5245

Printed and bound in the United States of America.

16 15 14 13 12 11 10   1 2 3 4 5 6 7 8 9 10

LIBRARY OF CONGRESS CATALOGING-IN-PUBLICATION DATA

Oughourlian, Jean-Michel.
[Genèse du désir. English]
The genesis of desire / written by Jean-Michel Oughourlian ; translated by
Eugene Webb.
    p. cm.
Includes bibliographical references and index
ISBN 978-0-87013-876-8 (pbk. : alk. paper)
1. Married people—Psychology. I. Title.
BF575.D4O9213 2007
158.2—dc22
                                2009015649

Book and cover design by Sharp Des!ns, Lansing, MI

g green
press
ɪɴɪᴛɪᴀᴛɪᴠᴇ
Michigan State University Press is a member of the Green Press
Initiative and is committed to developing and encouraging eco-
logically responsible publishing practices. For more information about the Green
Press Initiative and the use of recycled paper in book publishing, please visit *www.
greenpressinitiative.org.*

Visit Michigan State University Press on the World Wide Web at:
www.msupress.msu.edu

To René Girard, both mentor and friend

Contents

Acknowledgments

It is to René Girard that I owe the desire that has animated me for thirty years and has given me the energy necessary to my research in psychological theory as well as in clinical psychology. I openly recognize this desire as mimetic.

I am also indebted to Girard for teaching me how to read the great texts of literature and philosophy without being intimidated by them, and with a joyous irreverence, enabling me to develop a new understanding of the theories I have read and the phenomena I have observed.

For some years, absorbed in my clinical activity and my teaching responsibilities, I have published little except articles in scientific periodicals. It was Girard again who introduced me to Benoît Chantre, whose heartening friendship encouraged me and kept me company throughout the writing of this book.

My work on this book has also benefited from the attentive and demanding collaboration of Jeanne Barzilaï, who has helped me to clarify and give shape to my ideas.

As far as the English translation is concerned, I am deeply grateful to my friend Eugene Webb, who had already translated my book *The Puppet of Desire,* making it available to the American public, and who also very kindly agreed to translate the present book. Eugene's work is more than a translation, because he has added to the original text much of his experience and his great intellectual rigor. I also wish to express my appreciation to my friend Trevor Merrill for his constant support and for compiling the index. Trevor is a brilliant scholar, totally bilingual, and certainly the most knowledgeable in mimetic research among the younger Girardians.

I have also been formed by all those who have taught me, corrected me, inspired me, and directed me during my life, by successive identifications, first with my parents, then with my teachers and with all those close to me, and also with the friends who have influenced me. Each of them has become a part of me, and each lives in my appreciative and affectionate memory.

Introduction

I have been practicing as a psychiatrist for forty years. My professors taught me, during my internship and clinical residency, to diagnose pathologies of mood and temperament (mania, melancholy, depression of various types), of personality (psychoses and neuroses), and of behavior (sexual, eating, social, etc.). I learned, like all my colleagues, to treat these with medications. There can be no doubt that psychopharmacology has made extraordinary progress during these last forty years, revolutionizing our view of mental illnesses and especially our ways of handling them and our ideas about their prognoses.

During my years of clinical practice, however, something became obvious to me: in addition to the patients who came to me seeking help for an *illness* that could be clearly categorized and treated with an appropriately specific therapeutic technique, an increasing number came for some *problem* that was poisoning their lives but which definitely did not derive from a mental illness.

I soon realized that these problems were not simply located within the patient but were situated between the patient and some *other*: father, mother, brother, sister, partner, boss, employee, associate, and so on. The problems that were the most common and the most toxic for physical and psychic health were those afflicting couples, and I found myself at a loss as to how to resolve them.

Certainly many couples were flourishing; fifty years after their initial falling in love, numerous couples are still together and remain very happy. Of course couples such as those do not come seeking help. Those who do come to a therapist, either together or separately, are those who have run into difficulties. These often find themselves victims of a paradox: that the very desire that originally drew them to each other and brought them into union has mysteriously transformed into a force that separates them as violently as it once united them.

Consequently, I have devoted my theoretical and clinical research for the last twenty years to the effort of analyzing these phenomena. René Girard's theory of mimetic desire provided precious clues for understanding them. Beginning in 1996, the discovery of mirror neurons has also brought experimental evidence regarding the underlying mimetic mechanisms and provided scientific verification of their reality, so that they are no longer simply hypothetical assumptions but proven facts. The director of the Center for Brain and Cognition at the University of California, San Diego, Vilayanur Ramachandran, writes:

> I predict that mirror neurons will do for psychology what DNA did for biology: They will provide a unifying framework and help explain a host of mental abilities that have hitherto remained mysterious and inaccessible to experiments.[1]

Drawing on the intuitions of thinkers, philosophers, and psychologists, and applying the already developed theory of mimetic desire along with the new, remarkable discovery of mirror neurons, I have tried to understand better what it is that both unites and separates couples. I have discovered that it is the working of one and the same mimetic mechanism that creates first love and then hatred, that draws couples together and then drives them apart—a mechanism of which they are the playthings. My purpose in this book is to show that there are strategies for escaping the power of this mechanism, strategies that can be effective but that require the partners—or at least one of them—to become aware of the mimetic mechanism that manipulates them, and to be willing to make the effort, and sometimes even the sacrifices, needed for avoiding its harmful effects.

*   *   *

Marina, a twenty-five-year-old model, was sent to me by a colleague whom I greatly respect and who urged me to accept her as a patient. She entered my office in tears, overcome with emotion, without makeup, with her hair disheveled, wearing a jogging suit.

She said, "Something absolutely horrible has happened to me. I've been living in London for three years with a sixty-year-old man—intelligent, with many women, a millionaire, and an able and successful businessman. For my sake he divorced his wife of thirty years, something he never did for any of his previous mistresses. He was torn between me and a young, twenty-year-old, Swedish model, but he finally chose to live with me. My parents, of whom I am very fond, know nothing about this relationship. It would kill them; they're very conservative and want me to have a normal life, with a husband and children. They've wondered what I've been doing in London, but I told them I was working. Actually, I was living on money that Eddy gave me. Then six months ago, Eddy got prostate cancer. I accompanied him to the hospital for his treatment, and I stuck with him through his chemotherapy. But all hope of having a child with him disappeared, and I could see clearly that there was no future for us. I told Eddy that. He was very understanding and suggested I go to Paris for a couple of weeks to think about it and visit with my parents.

"Then a few days after I arrived in Paris, I met Hubert, who is thirty-five years old, handsome, charming, athletic, and the head of his own business. He fell in love with me and wanted to meet my parents, who were delighted with him. To them he seemed the perfect son-in-law."

"Does Hubert love you?" I asked her.

"Oh, yes! He's talking about getting married."

"And do you love him?"

"Yes, I love him, I admire him, I appreciate him, but I'm not exactly in love. I can't get over Eddy. When I talk on the phone with Eddy, he understands me, he comforts me, he even gave me his approval regarding this—and I start to cry. When Hubert tells me he loves me, I cry then too. I feel lost. I no longer know what I want or what I ought to do."

"How long have you and Hubert been together?"

"For about a month."

"And you've been crying nonstop for the whole month?"

"More or less. In fact, it got a lot worse eight days ago when Eddy, on the phone, advised me to choose Hubert. He told me that he loved me enough to tell me that and to put my interest and my future above everything. He said that he was himself going to return to his previous girlfriend, Ingrid, and go away with her to the Caribbean to try to console himself. During the whole conversation I couldn't stop crying; I had a lump in my throat and another one in my stomach, my hands were sweating. Part of the time now I have chills, and part of the time hot flashes; I can't eat any more, and I've lost almost seven pounds. Can you help me?"

*   *   *

Let us consider another case. Françoise comes into my office and looks at me unhappily.

"It's more than I can bear. I've been married to Lucien for twenty-five years, and we have three children. Then about a year ago I discovered he has a mistress."

"How did you find out?"

"Poking around in his computer with the help of my daughter. We found their email correspondence."

"Have you spoken with him about it?"

"I certainly have. But he denies it, and we argue about it endlessly. If only he had the courage to admit the truth, but he refuses and tells me I'm crazy. And that *really* drives me crazy. I'm depressed, I've lost my appetite, I wake up in agony every couple of hours."

"I'd like to talk with your husband."

"He won't tell you anything. I can't even recognize him anymore. He's become a monster; he used to be so nice . . ."

Lucien comes into my office with an air of hesitancy. He looks wary, as if he thinks I've already judged him. He launches an attack: "My wife probably told you I'm a louse. I hate her for talking to everyone about it, but above all I hate her for having dragged our daughter into our marital problems. She's taken her mother's side; she won't even speak to me. Since you're bound to medical confidentiality, I'll tell you right out: yes, I have a mistress, a woman who understands me and appreciates me, while my wife has been jumping on me for this and for that for years and calls me all sorts of names, especially when she's drunk."

"Oh, she drinks?"

"She sure does, and for a long time now. It's gotten worse over the years. Often when I come home in the evening I've found her on the floor. She's no longer the woman I married. She makes me think of that song by Aznavour: she's like her mother, she lets herself go to pieces. She's drinking more and more, and she cries all the time, about anything at all. I go to my girlfriend to get a little peace, but she's found out about her, and now I don't know what to do any more. I can't recognize her any longer. How could I have married her?"

"I'm going to talk with her again."

Françoise comes in with a triumphant air:

"So you've seen the jerk? I'll bet he's told you a bunch of lies."

"You didn't tell me you had a drinking problem. Your husband thinks that's an important issue."

"Yes, I drink to console myself for being treated the way I've been treated. Do you know that for years we've had no sexual relations? Now I know why. What bothers me the most is that his mistress is exactly my age. If he'd just taken some young thing, I could understand. And he even has the nerve to tell me that he doesn't sleep with her, that he only talks with her!"

"To sum it up then, your husband says that he's drifted away from you over the years because of your drinking. And you say that you drink because he has a mistress . . ."

I note in my file: "Impossible to judge. Impossible to determine the causality. What to do? See the husband again . . ."

*   *   *

Véronique is a beautiful woman around thirty or so, a high-powered accountant, visibly energetic and responsible. But when she sits down across from me, she seems lost and doesn't know where to begin.

She gets hold of herself and says, "I've been married for seven years. My husband is an expert on contemporary art. We have two children. We have been and still are in love with each other. He's a wonderful man. For several years, in fact from the very beginning, he's always been jealous. He suspects me of being interested in every friend he introduces to me; he reproaches me if I dress too well when going to work, saying that I'm doing it in order to seduce my colleagues or my clients. I used to laugh about it and took it as an indication of his love for me, and I think maybe it was. But in the last six months he's changed. He doesn't want to make love with me any more unless I tell him I've been to bed with Pierre, Paul, or Jacques. He begs me to tell him what it was like, what they did. I told him that there's nothing to say, because nothing happened, and then he said something that just threw me for a loop: 'Then make something up! It's my fantasy. And if you don't want to make it up, take a lover and tell me about it.' What do you think of that? He's gone crazy; he wants to get rid of me. I love him, and he tells me that if I love him, I ought to take a lover to please him, so that we can recover the joy of making love . . . I feel confused. I talked to one of my women friends about it, and she's the one who gave me your address."

* * *

Virginia is a charming young woman, about forty years old. Unmarried now, she has a boutique in the suburbs that sells women's clothing. When she was twenty-five, she married an older man, then lost him to cancer about five years later. She has no children, and she had no relationships until the day when . . .

"I met Pierre when he came into my shop to buy a dress for his wife for their anniversary. I could see right away that he was married, and yet when that big, handsome, blue-eyed man invited me to lunch, I said yes. We started meeting more and more often for lunch or for dinner, and he talked about his wife, who he said was half crazy, who was hospitalized, who was getting better, but who was sick, whom he couldn't leave alone but also couldn't bear any longer. And then one day he invited me to go away with him for the weekend; his wife was with their daughter in Brittany. I accepted.

"Since then it's been a living hell. Pierre moved in with me, carrying his bags and all his stuff. We bathed in bliss for a few weeks. Then he became somber, he phoned his wife more and more frequently, until one day he told me he couldn't abandon her, that she couldn't get along all by herself, that he felt guilty. So he packed up his bags again and went home. I wept for eight days. Then Pierre started calling me again and again, telling me that his life was unbearable, that his wife was impossible, and that he loved me, and only me, that I was the woman of his life. Until finally, one day, he was at my door with his bags and I took him in again . . ."

She burst into tears and ended by saying, "He left me again yesterday, bags and all, for the eighth time! Can you believe it? I'm going crazy. What does he want? What should I do? Have you ever heard such a story?"

"I have indeed!" I answered. "I call it 'the yo-yo husband.' The story isn't over yet either."

* * *

Fabienne is a slender young woman, thirty-six years old. Married for six years, she has two children, a two-year-old and a three-year-old. She waited a long time to have children because she was working, but eventually she went ahead, urged by the affectionate pressure of her parents, her friends, and her husband.

Fabienne and her husband work for the same company. Her husband, a hard worker, advanced from promotion to promotion and now he heads the office. She, on the other hand, held back, she says, by the work of the household and the birth of her first child, never received a promotion and finally quit. Her husband consoled her, saying he was making enough money for the family to live on and that she could devote herself to the role of mother and homemaker.

"That looks good on paper," Fabienne tells me, "but I'm not happy. I don't really miss my job, but housework doesn't interest me. I must confess that I'm not interested in my children either. They exhaust me. Their crying gives me a headache. My husband helps give them their baths at night, but he comes home later and later. He works too much. I know that it's for our sake he's working, but even to think about that exasperates me. On weekends I'm so worn out that I stay in bed while my husband looks after the children. Then he gets worn out too. The reason I've come to see you is that I'm having terrible headaches, I can't sleep, and I'm weighed down by an immense fatigue that never lets up. I no longer have any desire to make love with my husband. I feel nervous and irritable."

I ask to meet with her husband, and when he comes into my office what I see is a young man who seems a nice person but who looks deeply discouraged. "Yes, I know," he says, "I do everything I can, but nothing works. The children are uncontrollable and more than one can bear. My wife is tired all the time and frazzled. There's nothing that pleases her. Do you think she might be suffering from depression? As for me, I'm at the end of my tether; I find myself wondering if I should just give up, quit my job, and stay home to take care of my wife and children."

I answer that that needs thinking over; we should both think about it and meet again. It is clear that here, too, a mechanism is at work that is in the process of destroying the marriage. But we know that psychological tensions and stress can bring with them physical and psychosomatic symptoms of all sorts. If the husband keeps on exhausting himself, he'll be at risk for an embolism or a heart attack, but if he renounces all his ambitions in order to turn himself into a nursemaid, God only knows what kind of effect this might have on his total organism. I experienced that with Frederick.

*   *   *

Frederick, a cordial gentleman, is about sixty years old. He has nervous crises. I was urgently summoned to his hospital room. I found him rolling on the floor, shouting that he was in agony and that he couldn't bear to live any longer. With him was his very pretty wife, twenty-five years younger than he. Looking up at me in fear and bewilderment, she said, "I understand how Frederick feels. He has terrible problems. Anyone would be in his state." Dumbfounded, I asked her, "What sort of problems?"

"Money problems. Frederick was a millionaire when I met him. We fell in love and married. Then he made some bad investments and lost everything. I had to resume my former work as a secretary in order to make something for us to live on. His sister, however, preserved her share of their inheritance, and she's paying his hospital bills."

At that moment, Frederick sat up, calmed down a bit, put himself together, and said, "Doctor, a few years ago I almost bought Disneyland. But now I don't even have enough money to buy a ticket to visit it for a day."

Frederick has further symptoms: he goes through periods of confusion in which he doesn't know what he is saying or doing; he stumbles around as though drunk and falls into crises like the one I had just witnessed. There seems only one hope for him: that he can somehow find in himself the necessary inner resources to start again—what my friend, the well-known French psychiatrist Boris Cyrulnik, calls "resilience," so that he can rebuild his career and his fortune. For that he is going to need his wife to be a faithful ally.

* * *

The examples I have just gone over, and the hundreds of others that I could recount from my career, have raised searching questions and forced me to delve into a variety of disciplines in order to find answers. All of these patients shared certain characteristics:

- None of them was suffering from any standard mental illness.
- All had some problem that was spoiling their lives.

In order to explain their problem and the solutions I tried to bring to it, I am first going to have to ask the reader to accompany me through an account of a journey of discovery that began for me when I met René Girard in 1971. He or she will have to delve with me into Girard's mimetic theory of human motivation to see how it casts a new light on the human sciences.

At the time I met Girard I had an initial intuition, which was that although individuals like these had problems, what was "sick" was neither the one nor the other of the protagonists, but the *relation* that linked them. What I came to understand was that the crucial factor in that relation was each one's desire—understood in the broad sense of psychological movement—a desire that is essentially mimetic.

Before undertaking that theoretical exploration, however, I would like to recount one last conversation with a patient, Martha. This elegant woman of around sixty or so came into my office and looked at me in some embarrassment. "I don't know if I'm doing the right thing in coming to you," she said. "I'm not really sick. There's nothing in particular bothering me; I don't feel pain anywhere. It's just that I'm becoming impossible. I annoy my husband, constantly keeping after him out of jealousy. Although we're never apart, I can't stand it when he even looks at other women. He can't help doing so, and that causes painful tension between us, which I know is stupid, because we love each other and we have every reason to be completely happy."

"Does he look at all other women?"

"Yes, and it gets to me. Even if he looks too attentively at a movie or television actress, I make a scene about it."

"It must be a living hell for your husband."

"Yes, and for me too, since I blame myself. At bottom, I know it's stupid . . ."

"No, it's not stupid, it's just mechanistic. Consider this: do you like animals?"

"I adore them. I especially adore my cat, who is the love of my life. We have no children, and the cat takes their place, in a way. To give you an idea, the other day he got his head stuck between the slats of our balcony and I nearly had a heart attack."

"Because you love your cat, you love cats in general, wouldn't you say?"

"Yes."

"And when you see a cat in the street, you look at it, you stop, you even try to pet it."

"Yes."

"And what does that indicate? That attitude, the interest and spontaneous affection you feel for all cats and even for dogs, and which extends in a way to all animals, points to just one fact: that you adore your cat."

"Certainly."

"But you wouldn't exchange your cat for any of the ones you see, even if one of them was younger or better looking."

"Absolutely not."

"What would you say if your own cat made a scene every time you petted another cat?"

"But he does! If he sees me pet another cat, he jumps, he becomes upset. That's why I never do that when he's around."

"Do you see any similarity between the relationship you have with your cat and the one you have with your husband?"

She laughs. "Yes, I see what you mean." A patient's laugh is a good sign in psychotherapy; it indicates a realization, and also mutual understanding between the patient and the therapist.

"If your husband didn't love you, he wouldn't be interested in women and wouldn't look at them. He looks at them in your company because you're always together, and if he didn't love you, he probably would have left you, considering all you've put him through."

"Yes, he's even told me that he's not going to be able to take it much longer. But what can I do?"

"You can take hold of his desire and shape it yourself by calling his attention to pretty women to look at. When he sees a pretty woman, his interest will be aroused, and his desire will start to take shape. If you try to forbid his desire, you'll run the risk of reinforcing it. But on the other hand, if you keep him company in it, he'll love you all the more, and his desire will turn back toward you."

A few days later, Martha comes to see me again. "I've been thinking a lot about what we talked about the other day. And I tried what you suggested. And it works! My husband is so surprised that I'm no longer trying to catch him out. I even tell him to look at some pretty girl who's just come into a restaurant. The other day he hugged me and gave me a kiss, and that same afternoon he bought me a dress, saying he'd found me again. But I'm still having a hard time understanding what it's all about."

"You react each time he looks at a woman, as if he's already run off with her, and you now understand that that's excessive. What's really going on in your mind at that moment? You interpret every woman as a rival, and you immediately enter into conflict with her, demanding that your husband choose: her or you! You can see how you're devaluing yourself when you do that; you're putting your claims as a wife at risk in competition with the first woman who comes along."

Martha is what I call a patient of good faith. She listens, she wants to understand, she wants to learn, she sees me as an ally, a counselor, not an enemy. That is why her problem could be resolved. It doesn't always go like that with patients. Many of them are of bad faith; they come to a consultation in order to checkmate their therapist and add him to their long list of victims.

If one wants to make things clear to a patient and avoid such a rivalrous and sterile duel, one must explain from the start that there are three poles present in the consulting office: the patient on one side, the rivalrous desire or neurosis on the opposite side, and finally the therapist between the two.

One must ask if the patient wishes to join as a team with the therapist against the patient's problem (in fact, that is, against his desire)—the desire that holds him, that directs him, the rivalrous desire that one may call his neurosis—or on the other hand, if he wishes to ally himself with the neurosis against the therapist.

The time has come for us to talk about desire and begin what one might call the long initiatory journey that I myself went through and from which I came out transformed. The reader who makes the effort to follow me will live through the same experience.

*   *   *

I have always thought that desire is the heart and the energy of the relation to the other, the first movement that carries us toward life. My years of research and clinical observation have convinced me that that it is indeed desire that humanizes us, that impels us to unite with each other, to associate with each other, to assemble into groups, and also, as we will see, to *resemble* each other. It forms us in proportion as it animates us and arouses our thoughts and feelings. Desire leads us to seek out the company of others, their approval, their friendship, their support, and their recognition. But this can also be accompanied by rivalry and hatred; it can arouse both love and violence. Desire can be our greatest ally but also our worst enemy, driving us to wish for what will destroy us, to pursue what will cause us suffering, while we remain unable to understand it or figure out why it is happening. How does desire take shape? Where does it get its energy? The widespread romantic illusion always wants to think that our desire is autonomous, springing from within ourselves, that it is our own exclusive property. And this belief, despite recent remarkable advances in psychology and neurobiology, seems compelled to resist all the new knowledge that gives it the lie. "It is easier to split an atom," said Einstein, "than to break through a prejudice," and he knew more than anyone else what prodigious energy is needed to split an atom.

I quickly embraced the theory of mimetic desire as set forth by Girard in his *Deceit, Desire, and the Novel,* which claimed that every desire we have is copied from that of another person.[2] I was immediately impressed by the explanatory power of that theory, and I subsequently joined forces with Girard and with Guy Lefort in developing its application to psychology and psychiatry. *Things Hidden since the Foundation of the World* (1978) presented our initial reflections.[3] My own subsequent book, *The Puppet of Desire* (1982), proposed a phenomenology of mimetic desire as I had observed it, especially as it related to the phenomena of hysteria, possession, and hypnosis.[4] Since then, I have continued my efforts to work out a method of therapy that takes into account the fundamental "otherness" of desire, and I have now developed this approach sufficiently to present the results in a new book.

Over the years, my clinical practice as a psychiatrist has enabled me to assess the great therapeutic value of the mimetic theory. Every day I find myself amazed by its power to elucidate complex situations that might at first seem simply irrational. And I still feel surprised to see how many troubled couples are really prisoners of that mimetic mechanism working in them without their awareness. Jealousy, lust, rivalry, indifference can work their way into the heart of a relationship by way of the very force of desire that brought them together in the first place. How can we understand such a strange paradox?

The true nature of desire, its *mimetic* character, along with our denial of that truth, leads us ceaselessly to copy within ourselves the desires of everyone we encounter, subjecting ourselves to their influence, and by that very act of imitation, making them into rivals and indeed obstacles to the fulfillment of what we think are our own desires. The endless antagonism growing out of our claim to the supposed originality and spontaneity of our desires, and therefore to our personal autonomy, nurses continually our feelings of rivalry and our will to dominate and coerce.

The other essential truth about desire is therefore that *rivalry is always connected with it:* because I desire the same thing as the other and deny his claim to be the origin of that desire, I make him my rival, and as this rivalry takes shape, I am led to desire all the more what he desires and to try to take it away from him. In this manner desire and conflict escalate.

When the rivalry increases to the point that the subject is no longer interested in anything but the rivalry itself, we find ourselves in the domain of psychopathology. Unable to take possession of the very being of the person he imitates, the subject, in a sort of vengeful transference, launches into an attack on his person or on some object that stands for him. The "illness," therefore, is not situated either in the subject or in his rival but rather in the relation that binds them together.

Most of the pathologies I encounter in clinical practice (hysterias, phobias, anxieties, destructive passions, obsessional jealousies, anorexias, and so on) are illnesses of desire, as I will proceed to explain. When the rivalry induced by mimetic desire binds us too intensely to a series of models, we become enslaved by these relationships of hostility. Our failure to understand our mimetism condemns us to remain perpetually bound to the same destructive models and gradually to become strangers to ourselves and to those we love. Instead of allowing the underlying, ever changing otherness that inevitably constitutes us to flow freely, we remain fixated on the same impossible models and do not allow ourselves to be carried along further toward others on whom we might be able to model ourselves benignly.

The purpose of mimetic psychotherapy is to release people who are bound up in those types of endless rivalry, to gradually unmask and unravel their illusory attachments and make them free to choose other models. Once our tendency to imitate is recognized as such and accepted, it can itself liberate us and protect us instead of enslaving us.

* * *

It is through research, practice, and clinical observation that I have come to understand that all human relations are governed by one and the same principle: a "universal mimesis," from which no one can extricate himself and which operates in us inexorably. It is the nature itself of our desire that makes us imitate one another ceaselessly and remain always under the influence of those around us.

The recent discovery of mirror neurons, to which I will devote one entire chapter, provides decisive confirmation of this hypothesis about human nature and opens significant possibilities for research into the way this universal mimesis functions at the level of the nervous system. Mirror neurons are triggered automatically in our brains not only when we carry out any action ourselves, but also whenever we witness another performing some action or showing an intention to do so. It is quite astonishing. It appears that we are constantly in mimetic interaction with one another from the very moment of birth. Thus we can see empathy grounded in scientific fact. The emotions and judgments that accompany the firing of these neurons correspond to the instant reverberation of mirror neurons in the limbic system and the cortex. This seems to indicate that it is not our ideas and feelings that determine our behavior, but rather one and the same mimetic mechanism that determines all three.

All human thoughts and feelings, in their innumerable diversity, would thus seem to be colorations of this mechanism that characterizes the field of human being in its entirety. This does not detract in any way from their richness, their complexity, their sparkling flux; the principle that governs them is one, but the multiplicity of their forms remains unlimited. Universal mimesis, in the same manner as the principle of universal gravitation, can explain innumerable different phenomena. Combining attraction and repulsion, it pulls people together while also keeping them separate. It is, as we shall see, the principle that both individualizes us and universalizes us, just as it also binds us and at the same time gives us liberty. Mimesis, therefore, is a profoundly ambiguous force. We only need to understand its mechanisms so that we will no longer be its passive playthings but become able to take control of it and direct its energy.

For some, such a theory seems difficult to accept. Its clarity and simplicity, its cross-disciplinary character, and the complexity and contradictoriness of the phenomena it is able to explain all by itself may motivate the resistance the mimetic theory sometimes encounters. It nevertheless applies to everyone, clearly manifesting itself in our daily lives. Perhaps one reason it is so often misunderstood is due to one of its most perplexing paradoxes: it is because we are all imitating each other constantly that we are able to be who we are! The otherness and the mobility of our desire, with its continually mirroring transformations, are in reality the guarantee of our endless capacity to learn and become ourselves; they are the source of our possibility of transcending a predetermined nature that would enclose us in a fixed and final selfhood.

To clarify further the notion of mimetic desire, I will offer a reading of the Book of Genesis, which I think shows more clearly than any other story that it is within the heart of our relationships, in the act of exchange and by the dynamism of mimetic desire, that a human being is born into psychological life and becomes aware of himself or herself. It is here that one's identity and one's individuality are forged. It is also by the very nature of that desire, tied up as it always is with rivalry, that one is cast into the "world of fallenness," leaving behind the paradise of love and of joyous fullness. If we are to recover our first innocence, those initial sparks of love, we will have to undo the illusions that desire is so quick to give birth to: the illusions of our autonomy and of our radical difference from others, with all the other false differences that this idea brings along with it. We must do this in order to come to know the otherness that runs through our very being and continually works changes in us.

Finally, I will present a study of the psychology and psychopathology of rivalry and of couples that a mimetic perspective enables us to approach in a manner that is original and, in my opinion, especially practical and effective. I will suggest some strategies for helping a couple to escape a spiral of rivalry in which they may find themselves being swept along. To allow love to unfold, a couple has to learn to defuse the rivalry that threatens their relationship in every moment. And the sort of day-to-day asceticism this must involve requires a clear understanding of the mimetic mechanisms that are always working to undermine love and pervert it.

Armed, then, after these theoretical excursions, with the necessary theoretical equipment and initiated into the ploys of mimetic desire and rivalry, the reader will learn, and be able to understand, the outcome of the stories of Marina, Françoise, Véronique, and the rest.

CHAPTER 1

Psychological Movement

1. MIMETIC DESIRE

*Men think themselves free simply because they are conscious of their actions and
ignorant of the causes by which they are determined.*

—Spinoza

To be able to reflect on desire, I propose to give it a definition that seems
to me both appropriate and sufficiently broad to allow investigators from a
variety of fields to think about it together: *desire is psychological movement.* In
psychology, there is no movement that is not desire, and there is no desire
that is not movement.

Every movement requires an *energy,* a "driving force." It also supposes a
finality, that is, a *goal* toward which its trajectory can be oriented—some object,
an idea or an ideal that can order it, attract it, give it definiteness. The great
psychological theories (psychoanalysis, behaviorism, cognitive psychology)
have taken positions regarding that energy and that finality and have attrib-
uted to them various origins and explanations.

For my part I became convinced early on of the tremendous power of the
theory of mimetic desire. This theory takes its departure from a very simple
anthropological hypothesis: that a person's desire is always copied from the
desire of somebody else. To put this another way, this means that our desires

17

do not belong to us, that they are not determined by some special property of our own but are suggested to us by another person whom we rush to imitate. When I fall in love, it is only myself believing that my desire has spontaneously surged toward this woman who suddenly seems to me unique among all others. I believe that I alone perceive those hidden treasures in her that escape all others. In reality, however, if I recognize this woman as special, separating her out from all those around her—who may, after all, be no less desirable—it is not because I divine in her secret qualities or ideal virtues that my perspicacity alone has made known to me. Nor is it that she alone is capable of striking a resonant chord in my being, but rather that she corresponds to a whole series of cultural "models" that have been presented to me over the years and have tutored me regarding "whom to desire."

Usually this mediation is even more direct: it passes by way of the desire of somebody close to me who has pointed her out without even realizing it. Some friend has called my attention to her beauty or has commented on her charm, her obvious attractiveness, her intelligence. And whatever I may think about that person, whether I simply feel some esteem for him, or whether he may even be my best friend, his revealing that he feels attraction to her awakens my curiosity, arouses a similar interest and soon elicits a similar sense of attraction in me, an attraction that I believe is spontaneous, despite the role of the other's mediation in giving birth to it. That is why it is possible to fall in love with a person one may not yet even have met—by hearing others talk about her, praising her qualities in terms that sound charged with desire and that by that very fact evoke desire. When I do meet her, then, I will already, without realizing it, be predisposed to fall in love with her.

Or I might also fall in love out of rivalry. Whether intentionally or not, my beloved may forbid me to love her while at the same time encouraging me to do so by her own behavior. In the midst of passionate kissing, she may say, "You mustn't love me. I am already engaged—alas—to someone else. He loves me and wants to marry me. I didn't yet know you when I promised myself to him. I can't destroy him by abandoning him, still (accompanied by another passionate embrace), alas, it's you that I love. But our love is impossible."

This sort of situation is not uncommon, and one who takes part in such a conversation can feel his (or her) desire surge like a lightning bolt due to the action of two mechanisms that we will encounter again and again in the course of our study:

(1) the interdiction: our love is impossible;
(2) the presence of a rival.

As Corneille might say, "pierced to the heart by a blow as unexpected as it is deadly,"[1] the one who hears these words between two ardent kisses will, from that time on, have as his (or her) single goal in life to smash that interdiction, to defeat that rival, and to take possession, through marriage, of that so unique and so precious object.

It is not so much love that is blind but the desire that carries it, because that desire is always drawn by the desire of others rather than by the object it pursues. The same is true of fashions in clothing, of fashionable ideas, or of what is "politically correct"—all are examples of mimetic desire at work.

Some years ago I asked Yves Saint-Laurent how he was able to be sure that the dresses he designed would accord with the taste of the public. He looked at me, clearly surprised at my ignorance of such a simple psychological fact, and answered, "But Doctor, they will wear what I like!" The techniques of suggestion and of manipulation of mimetic desire were being used by advertising long before having been analyzed and proven by psychologists, and with a degree of success that anyone can see.

A Chameleon Desire

If every desire we have has been suggested to us, the obvious corollary is that we can scarcely lay claim to our prior ownership of it, and still less can we claim spontaneity and originality for it. Every desire is born from a relationship; it emerges from within it. And it can take innumerable forms that can never be determined in advance. Desire can bear upon any object, any being, any idea, any project that may have been singled out by some other person. The mimetic nature of desire is paradoxically bound up with its freedom: it never has a determinate identity of its own, but is always ready to follow after any other that crosses its path.

What other? Every other—all those around us whom we take as models, whether they are intimates or strangers, whether because we feel an inner attraction to them or because we feel esteem for them, anyone we compare ourselves to, anyone whose superior qualities we recognize and would like to have for our own. In this sense, mimetic desire is always a desire "to be," to exist in greater measure, a desire for an achievement or a dreamed-of completeness that one might feel stands before one but is being held onto by the other. In the innumerable encounters that constellate our lives, the infinite interactions of everyone with everyone else, we are thus entirely caught up in endless games of imitation—mimetic games that for the most part remain hidden from us, even though they are at the heart of our existence and of our relationships.

This is undoubtedly why this theory that is in principle so accessible and obvious sometimes runs up against so much incomprehension: it requires us to rethink in a most fundamental way the notions of the subject and of desire and, despite all our shared beliefs, to renounce the glorious but mythic autonomy with which we have adorned humanity—to renounce, too, the pleasure we experience through being the playthings of those hidden mechanisms.

When we go to the theater, we certainly have no wish to see the gears hidden behind the scenery; we prefer to surrender ourselves to the pretense of the representation and not let ourselves be distracted from the pleasant illusion in which we are immersed. And yet, we know that it is an illusion, and that knowledge does not prevent us from experiencing each time a renewed pleasure, becoming once again an enchanted spectator.

Desire, the Driving Force of Rivalry

One of the most important psychological effects of mimetic desire, and one of the most problematic and most prominent in clinical practice, is the rivalry that desire implacably generates. From the very fact that I imitate the desire of another, that I want to take for myself either what belongs to him or what he seeks to acquire, that other person appears to me an obstacle. The other intrudes himself between me and the object. I enter into competition with him. The model whose desire I borrow becomes my rival, but to a degree that varies extensively according to how closely he is involved with me and according to the nature of the object of the desire. René Girard speaks of "external mediation" when the model is at a distance, and therefore outside the range of direct competition, and "internal mediation" when the model is within that range.

If the model lives in a different world from mine, in another social sphere, he mediates my desire in a triangular pattern made up of subject, mediator, and object, but this has no effect on my relation to him, due to the fact that he is himself inaccessible to me and the object is also at a distance. Thus Don Quixote will be able to imitate an exalted literary figure like Amadis of Gaul, in the peaceful, admiring manner Cervantes describes. If, more modestly, I should take as model some political figure whom I have no opportunity to meet or become personally acquainted with, I can content myself with trying to resemble him by desiring everything he desires and that he can be; I may try to talk like him, to think like him, to dress like him, to copy the qualities I attribute to him—assurance, authority, altruism, fairness, determination, and so on—without ever being able to enter into real competition with him.

The imitation can therefore remain completely peaceful and benign. I don't mistake myself for him or try to take his place; I don't try to take his belongings away from him. I only try to draw nearer to him by resembling him. Such imitation, which is often consciously undertaken and amounts to a sort of identification with him, may lead me to become sensitive to social and political problems I had not understood until then, to commit myself to some sort of political action that will give meaning and a new dimension to my existence.

On the other hand, the closer the model is to me within my own world of activity and the more accessible the object of our desire, the more danger there is that it will arouse covetousness and rivalry in me. In such circumstances there can develop a sort of oriental politeness designed to adroitly deflect the rivalry incited by mimetic desire. This would demand that each of the two defuse every source of potential jealousy between them. If one of them says, "I think your necktie is beautiful," the other might immediately take it off and offer it to him. He would rather do without the necktie than have it become an object of contention. By giving away something belonging to him that has aroused the other's interest, he immediately placates the other's desire and avoids the mimetic rivalry the object could stir up. Women might do the same. If one says to another, "You have a beautiful scarf," the other might take it off and give it to her. Or if she is wearing something she can't take off and give away—some shoes, for example—she might say, "But they are yours, I'll make you a present of them," so as to undercut at the very moment of its birth any feeling of envy. Of course this requires self-control and a careful, ubiquitous, never ending asceticism. And it is often difficult in daily life to maintain this sort of constantly watchful attentiveness.

The Progressive De-differentiation of Rivals

When a budding rivalry is not deflected, defused, or avoided—for example, by attaching oneself to a different model—one can enter into a state of rivalrous reciprocity, that is, a rivalry that has a constant tendency to intensify: the mediator whose desire I imitate, imitates mine in turn, redoubling its ardor. I in turn, then, will desire all the more ardently the object he possesses, and so on. In such a game of symmetrical redoubling, each becomes a model-rival for the other. The mimetic triangle, subject-mediator-object, becomes transformed into a mimetic circle that becomes tighter and tighter, in the bosom of which desire circulates more and more rapidly and intensely, soon leaving both rivals facing off against each other.

In copying one another while drawing ever closer to each other, the rivals progressively become identical; little by little they come to have the same desires, the same gestures, the same aggressiveness, the same violence, the same obsession, to such an extent that nothing any longer really differentiates them in their actions and intentions. This becomes a sort of fusion in rivalry. Each then, in order to distinguish himself from the other, tries to denigrate his adversary, to triumph over him, to assert the anteriority of his own desire and his exclusive ownership of it. Both rivals fail to notice that in the midst of their opposition they have become interchangeable. Antigone alone announces this truth: there is no difference between her brothers Eteocles and Polynices, who have just killed each other in competition over the crown of Thebes. She denies that there is a good one and a bad one, a victor or a vanquished, and she upholds this truth at the risk of her life against the orders of Creon and his insistence on the political necessity of introducing a difference between them.

Desire Does Not Keep All Its Promises

In this gradual disappearance of the object as rivalry takes its place, another truth comes into view: if the subject succeeds in attaining the coveted object, the satisfaction he gets from it will be short-lived and is virtually guaranteed to be disappointing. Once the object is possessed, it will lose its glittering splendor. It will obviously fail to bring the increase in fullness of being, of enjoyment and power, that seemed to shine like a nimbus around the mediator. Still less will it bring the radical transformation that it seemed to promise—perhaps it will even bring the opposite of what it seemed to offer. "There are only two tragedies in life," wrote Oscar Wilde. "One is not getting what one wants, and the other is getting it." We spontaneously desire what others desire, simply because they desire it, but we do not understand that the realization of those desires will not necessarily assure our happiness. *be there are always more desires.*

Each of the rivals, completely preoccupied with the battle he is waging, fails to see that he has become a prisoner in a hell of rivalrous desire; when he thinks he's rising and drawing near to the hoped-for paradise, he plunges in the opposite direction into a descending spiral that carries him down into ever more hatred both of himself and of the other. Obtaining the object will not change anything. But instead of questioning the mechanism of the headlong rush in which he was ceaselessly transfiguring the object, he will turn toward some new good that he thinks will be able, this time, to fulfill his desire.

This bewildered chase risks making him run into checkmate again and again; believing himself to be approaching ever closer to a sovereign bliss that his victory over successive obstacles seems to guarantee, he charges blindly into increasing darkness.

The Increasing Exasperation of Desire

The de-differentiation and increasing exasperation that result from such mounting rivalry generate intense antagonism and lead in turn to what Girard calls a "mimetic crisis." The subject sees his rival as a cruel persecutor who wants to prevent him from gaining a perfect happiness. The initial rivalry becomes a ferocious, frenzied will to diminish the other no matter what the cost, to overturn him, crush him, cast him out, dominate him, even destroy him. Rivalry outraces the desire that gave birth to it. Thus one sinks into what in clinical terms I call pathological rivalry, something that happens particularly frequently and destructively in marriages, as we will see.

When desire arrives at this kind of mimetic paroxysm, it becomes transformed into what Girard calls "metaphysical desire." This savage, vampire-like desire separates us irremediably from the paradise we long for. Our feelings take on an extreme intensity; we want to melt into the other, take his place, rob him of his very being, of the secret of his luminous aura, of the autonomy that we dream of and that seems to be his. We want to dispossess him, which is to say, to possess him entirely. By taking possession of what the other *is*, the subject hopes to derive an increase of existence and of power that will guarantee him a final and exclusive happiness and the perfect enjoyment of his object. Acquiring the object is now only a means to acquiring the being of the mediator, which the subject has endowed with an imaginary prestige that one might even call a "hallucinatory sacrality." In sum, metaphysical desire is the expression of an imitation fixed upon a model on whom our desire is completely focused. Here imitation takes on increasingly problematic forms: unrestrained passions, destructive love, masochism and sadism, raging violence. Mimetic desire, normally so fluid in interaction with the flow of all the desires around us, begins to turn only about itself, like a broken record, bound to the circular rivalry that pulls it, unable to escape from its hypnotic attraction. It becomes obsessive and devouring. It loses its mobility, its natural changeableness, and can no longer succeed in moving on to gravitate around other models. The relationship becomes nothing but a reciprocal madness, a relationship hollowed out and reified by the rivalry that invades it.

Veneration and Hatred

When rivalry becomes this acute and invasive, when mimetic desire transforms into metaphysical desire, the "physical" object becomes remote, and it does so in inverse proportion to the closeness of the two rivals. The object soon becomes no more than simply a pretext for conflict. It becomes forgotten in favor of the rivalry itself, which comes to occupy the entire field between the two rival consciousnesses. The hatred one feels for one's mediator is often, in this process, only the reversed image of a fervent adoration, a secret adulation yoked to unconscious depreciation of oneself.

When a man begins to desire an inaccessible woman, whether she disdains him or belongs to another, real or imagined, this woman becomes simultaneously both the model of the desire she excites and its object; she inserts herself between the subject and the *being* that he thinks he sees her possess and that he would like to take to himself. She therefore becomes an obstacle to his reaching the qualities that she masks and he covets, and this very opacity endows her with an air of divinity. So he experiences for her a hopeless adoration that makes him swing back and forth between slavish abasement, veneration, and blind idolatry on the one hand—since compared with her, who is everything, he is nothing—and the most bitter hatred. It is she who excludes him from true life, from possible happiness, who reminds him constantly of his helplessness, his inferiority, his misery. He makes of her a monstrous and all powerful divinity, before whom he humbles and abases himself, whom he simultaneously adores and curses, unable to detach himself from her because he believes that through her he will find the hoped-for transformation of his existence.

The *Letters of a Portuguese Nun* describe with rare acuity these ravages of passion.[2] In love with an officer who has abandoned her, Marianne, a nun, writes to him, "I would much rather be wretched loving you than never to have seen you; I consent, therefore, without protest to my miserable fate, since you have not wished to make it a better one." She completely submits to the one who has left her, hands herself over to his will. She makes him into a god who has all power over her life. Because he partakes in her eyes of an enchanted transcendence from which she is hopelessly separated, her suffering, she believes, is clear proof of the superiority of that higher being she longs for. She cannot and does not wish to extricate herself from that suffering, because she believes it is the sign that she is near her god; if she is burning like this, it is because she is in contact with a too powerful radiance, because she is drawing near to a magical presence that would be capable ultimately of raising her on high. Her suffering becomes a substitute for the object she cannot attain; Marianne does not embrace the void, she embraces her suffering, and that very suffering functions as a bridge connecting her to the one she loves, serving to keep her united with him, to render him always present to her body, and to enable her to draw ever closer to him. The deeper she plunges into that pain, the more she can believe herself rising toward him and toward the light.

The Infernal Dimension of Desire

The increasing exacerbation of desire can heighten rivalry to the point that it can lead to a paroxysm of violence, to hatred, to physical aggression, even to murder. Here we discover the infernal face of desire that marks the loss of the paradise initially glimpsed and hoped for. The mechanism of mimetic desire can impel us toward beings or objects that are increasingly difficult to obtain and that will seem all the more seductive to us the more inaccessible they are. Coming up against a rival who obstructs it, insatiable desire can become endlessly intensified, becoming a gnawing pain, a self-alienation, a hopeless enslavement. Thus one can arrive at the most acute and terrifying form of passional pathology. As the reverse face of the paradisal, luminous fusion of love, hatred for one's model is the dead end of rivalrous fusion, the terrifying fall of desire into blind destruction, the monstrous inversion of love.

In Christian-Jaque's 1955 film version of Zola's *Nana*, Count Muffat realizes that Nana will never belong to him; having lost hope of ever possessing her, he strangles her, with the words, "You piece of trash, my love."[3] He dispossesses himself of her at the same time that he also dispossesses all possible rivals. At the height of the mimetic crisis, total contempt and absolute love blend together. Thus can metaphysical desire, the ultimate form of mimetic desire, lead us to desire "nothingness" and make murderers of us. It little matters what means we use to possess what we covet so avidly; if possession of the desired object proves impossible, we would rather destroy it so as to be certain that no one else will be able to possess it in our place. And we would be ready to destroy ourselves, if needed, in order to get at and destroy the other. Terrorism is an obvious manifestation of this sort of pathology.

Desires are always contagious: a copied desire transmits itself from person to person in a kind of mimetic epidemic. This social transmission increases the desire's intensity more and more as it passes from one to another, and also the love or the rivalry of which it is the bearer. Perhaps this is what explains the incredible magnetism exerted by certain public figures, such as famous actors or singers who become the objects either of fanatical adulation or universal condemnation. The same thing happens with fashions in clothing or with the social, cultural, ideological, or erotic fashions that take hold of society for a while and then pass; each indicates to his or her neighbors what is to be desired, and those in turn take up that desire and pass it along to everyone they meet, always believing that the desire has originated entirely with them.

When the contagion becomes not simply a fashion but a form of collective violence, the mimetic desire becomes transformed into a polarization of all against one: what had been an individual crime becomes a collective crime. That explains certain phenomena of mob psychology, which can be as sudden as they are unforeseen: lynchings, explosions of violence, running berserk, mass movements, or collective furies.

Desire, Need, and Instinct

It is also important to distinguish desire from need and from instinct, with which both of the first two are often confused.

Need preexists the object that will satisfy it. Hunger, for example, manifests itself before one finds whatever might appease it. Desire, however, is born at the same time as the object that is designated for it, that is, suggested to it. It is in the very moment I notice the existence of a woman toward whom someone has called my attention that I will suddenly find myself nursing an irrepressible desire for her, a desire that a few moments before did not even exist.

Need can be satisfied by any number of interchangeable objects. Thirst, for example, can be quenched by water, by milk, by fruit juice, by wine—it doesn't matter which. Desire, on the other hand, fixed since its birth on one object, cannot imagine being satisfied by any other. The object of desire can have no substitute; because it has been designated for me by the other whose desire I am copying, it cannot be changed. If I fall in love with the wife of my best friend, try as he might to shift my desire by showing me some other equally ravishing woman, she won't interest me, won't be able to substitute for her—unless my friend turns away from his wife himself to pursue another; then he may be able to reorient my desire, in company with his own.

When need is satisfied, it comes to rest, and its satisfaction is experienced as pleasure. Desire, on the other hand, knows neither satisfaction nor rest; pierced by the other's desire, it never stops but pursues its object tirelessly. It cannot extricate itself from the mimetism that never ceases to magnetize it. In his *Hallelujiah,* Georges Bataille writes, "The pursuit of pleasure is cowardly, it seeks simply to be appeased. Desire, on the contrary, is intent on never being extinguished."[4] Need makes us pass indifferently from one object to another and change our object when circumstances change, while desire is subject to mimetic necessity in its choice of object. Mimesis is a universal mechanism; none of us can escape it. But its necessity is not a simple determinism; I am still able to choose whom I wish to imitate and model myself on.

The discovery of mirror neurons confirms the mimetic hypothesis by bringing to light the neurological activity underlying mimetic desire, both in the individual who tries to appropriate an object and in the one who observes that act of appropriation. But I can also choose to resist being swept along by my desire, to let it flow through me without my submitting myself to its motion. If one of my desires begins to conflict with my convictions, I always retain the ability to reject it—not simply to follow it, but to choose another model. That often requires a clear understanding of the mechanisms that move us. But not always. Our desire, by its very nature, imitates all the desires around it. Now among all the desires we are susceptible to imitating, some contradict others, inviting us to follow very different paths; they can even lead us to pursue our own "interests," our "certainties," our "beliefs," that is, our cultural models (which are themselves, of course, acquired through imitation, education, and various forms of apprenticeship). We will therefore be led to reject one or another of these desires, since we cannot welcome them all simultaneously without being in contradiction with ourselves.

I was once present at a strange public session with some of my students. A great physician was hypnotizing a young psychoanalyst and telling her: "Your unconscious will furnish you with the answers you need to arrive at the results you wish." She immediately woke up from the hypnotic sleep in a panic. What happened? What jolted her out of the hypnosis so roughly? Her psychoanalytic education had taught her to associate the unconscious with a psychic power that plays dirty tricks on you; it was the source of all problems and all repressions. For the Ericksonian hypnotist, on the other hand, the unconscious represented a guardian angel who protects us, guides us, and shows us the way to make progress.[5] These two different theories of the unconscious clashed in the mind of the young woman. She did not recognize herself in the suggestion that was made to her and could not embrace the desire of the hypnotist. To her, the hypnotist was suggesting that she surrender herself to what she supposed was the anarchy of the unconscious and that she put herself in danger by doing so. Her psychoanalytic "cultural" model was in conflict with the model embodied here in the hypnotist. Just as any hypnotic subject can reject any hypnotic suggestion in favor of some other alternative—no hypnotist has ever been able to make a hypnotic subject into a murderer—we retain, even in the grip of the mimetic mechanism, our freedom.

This freedom is, of course, relative, since we can never escape the universal mechanism, but it nevertheless exists as freedom *of choice* among various possible imitations. I always have the possibility of choosing between different models, as well as among different suggestions by the same model. When our freedom of choice becomes shackled so that it can no longer exercise its liberty, that is a sign that rivalry has bound us too tightly to a single model who has become the focal point of all our attention and whose power of attraction we cannot pull loose from.

Need is biological. Desire is psychological. Need springs from within the biological constitution of the subject himself or herself. Desire, which is mimetic, derives its origin from the other. That having been said, one can imagine way stations and transitions between a pure, completely mimetic and psychological desire, such as the desire to win a literary prize, on the one hand, and on the other, a desire that "straddles" need; a mimetically derived desire to drink a great wine obviously would never take shape unless there was also an underlying physical need for liquid. Need is never disincarnate, separated from the biological, but desire often is.

Without mimesis, need is incapable of giving birth to a desire. Desire itself, however, can create a need. When passion grows between a man and a woman—in proportion, for example, as a third rival figure, real or imaginary, feeds jealousy and heightens desire—the lovers express themselves with a characteristic vocabulary: "I need you," "I can no longer get along without you," "I can't live without you," "I would be nothing without you," and so on. Here desire has created a quasi-physical need for the other, but a need that remains in reality a psychological desire. A person caught in the grip of this desire feels absolutely that he is incapable of getting along without the other, that he could not live without her, that it would be impossible to experience the absence of the object of his passion without dying.

All love songs speak of that sort of painful dependency, which has two striking consequences: if you are separated from the other, you think only of her; this becomes an obsession, and you want to recover her at any price. And if you see her again, you experience a renewed sense of missing her and of irrepressible need for her. It is a form of psychological addiction of the sort we find, interestingly enough, among drug addicts who take cocaine, one of the rare drugs that does not cause physical dependency. In American slang cocaine is called "the girl," because it creates within one the same imperious sense of inner craving as does being in love with a woman who "gets under your skin." The desire for it excites a truly burning feeling of need.

Need, on the other hand, cannot create desire. If we are not in love, a feeling of sexual need can be satisfied, in principle, by anyone—what is known as "the oldest profession in the world" stands ready to bear witness to this fact. But when our desire is fixated on someone who becomes our exclusive preoc-cupation, when all the energy of our need suddenly finds itself focused on that person alone, then only that person can assuage it. In this sense, need never creates all by itself a desire, even if desire can modify, pervert, or even create a need, so that obtaining sexual pleasure will be subject to certain imperious constraints—such as brunettes, blue shoes, or some particular scenario.

Instinct is a sequence of genetically determined behaviors. It ensures, in a cer-tain manner, the "stewardship" of need: hunger, the need to nourish oneself entails an instinctual set of acts that include chewing, swallowing, and so on, just as the sexual instinct governs the necessary details of copulation.

Instinct watches genetically and biologically over the successful carrying out of operations. It has no influence on desire. Desire, on the contrary, can have a determining influence on instinct and can even pervert it, for example, by modifying it so as to turn it away from nutrition—as when an anorexic, fixed on an ideal and impossible model, is no longer able adequately to nour-ish herself. All the various forms of sexual perversion (fetishism, voyeurism, sadomasochism, and so on) illustrate the myriad ways in which mimetic desire can modify the underlying sexual instinct. Animals have instincts and needs, but they do not have perversions—because they do not have desire.

Desire, then, which is energy and movement, is a force that, like any other, can manifest or exert itself only in the presence of some resistance. This resistance does not necessarily need to be real; it can also be imaginary. A perpetually jealous lover, always anxious about possible rivals who, for the most part, may not even exist, imagines all sorts of betrayals that torment him and make him more and more passionate and possessive. Every obstacle, even if only dreamed, feeds desire. If the resistance disappears or is withdrawn, the energy of passion fades; it can no longer exert itself or manifest itself. Similarly, desire cannot exercise its energy except in the presence of a resistance, and that energy increases in direct proportion to the strength of the resistance. On the other hand, if the resistance gives way, the desire dissolves into thin air.

This is what Valmont in *Les Liaisons dangereuses* writes to Madame de Tourvel in a cruel and deadly letter: "If I did love you once, I no longer love you. It's not my fault. . . . My love lasted as long your virtue did." I must also point out still another psychological truth expressed in his stunning statement "It's not my fault. . . ." Indeed, it is desire that both operates the self and creates it; the self is nothing but what one might call a "desire-self." The self as such, therefore, really isn't responsible: desire has followed its own destiny, its own logic; it disappeared as soon as the obstacle that put up resistance to it yielded. Here, the self recognizes that it has no power of its own and can do nothing!

Mimetic Escalation

Mimesis, the special form of unconscious imitation we have been analyzing, bears upon four aspects or attributes of the other, that is, of its model:

(1) *On his appearance,* that is, on what the other presents to be seen or heard. One can imitate the other's haircut, the trim of his beard, his gait, or his attitudes. One can also imitate his voice, the way the imitators do that we see on the stage or on television.

(2) *On his belongings.* This might be done nonviolently by going to purchase the same object that the star's publicity has told us he has. The star, with the prestige and fame he enjoys, confers his "aura" on the objects he possesses, the cars he drives, the clothing or accessories he wears. These objects are then sought out as carrying a surplus of "being." They appear to us as capable of giving us access to the higher realm the model has attained. But if my model is my near neighbor or someone in my circle of acquaintances, mimesis has no choice but to try to wrest his object away from him. Such "appropriative mimesis" entails conflict and violence.

(3) *On his being.* Imitation of the model's being can take two very different forms. One, as was explained above, is the violent, rivalrous form Girard calls "metaphysical desire," which consists of wanting to appropriate the substantial being of the model. Metaphysical desire is hellish and terrifying, in the sense that it can have catastrophic consequences, as much for the subject of desire as for his model-obstacle. This is a pathology that can lead to either suicide or murder.

Mimetic desire—by which we want what another wants—encompasses and contains the forms of mimesis that bear upon the appearance, the possessions, and the being of our model. It is a powerful, dreadful force that has a tendency constantly to goad itself further, leading to ever mounting rivalry. This can be understood as a kind of progressive hypnosis that sometimes becomes fatal.

The second form of imitation of the being of the other is pacific and constructive and permits us to avoid rivalry and conflict with the model: this is what I call "identification." Freud noticed this process and has written about it quite well.

I must, however, emphasize the continuity of this mechanism with the other dimensions of mimesis, as well as the fact that it employs a technique for the avoidance of violence and the construction of one's own identity that is widely used as a psychological strategy: by imitating the being of the model, I conform myself to him and recognize his part in the building up of my identity, which is nothing more than the sum of our successive identifications with all the models who have made us what we are.

When I identify myself with the model in this manner, I no longer feel any need to tear away from him his objects, his possessions, and his very being. I share with him a common identity, and I thereby escape from the violence of appropriative mimesis as well as from that of metaphysical desire.

(4) Last but not least, mimesis can bear on the desire of the other in its totality, and it can encompass and contain all the forms of imitation that have to do with the appearance, the possessions, and the being of the model.

2. Interdividual Psychology

Desire, the one and only mainspring of the world, desire, the only necessity man is compelled to experience.

—*André Breton*

Where does desire, that is to say, psychological movement, come from? Where does it get its energy? From the relation to the other. This relationship with the other seems to me so close and so fundamental that it should not be seen as merely a relation between two individuals, two subjects, but as a reciprocal movement of back and forth, carving out in each of its poles, by its very motion, an entity that can be designated as the "self." That is why Girard, Lefort, and I, in *Things Hidden since the Foundation of the World,* named the psychology of this relationship "interdividual psychology." We intended by this to found a new psychology, at the point of convergence of our psychological and anthropological research, that would no longer be a psychology of the individual or monadic subject, but rather a psychology of the relationship as such. It is the force of attraction exercised and undergone by each subject in relation to all others that supplies the psychological energy necessary for movement.[6] Mimetic desire does not draw its energy from anything except the relation to the other, from the interdividual relation. Both the movement produced and the energy that makes it possible stem from the same mechanism.

How does desire choose its object? How is the goal of this psychological movement determined? Since desire is mimetic, copied from the other's desire for what he possesses or is thought to possess, it receives from that other desire both its energy and its goal simultaneously. Mimesis, the universal principle of imitation of which we are unwittingly the playthings, guarantees the communication, the transfer of information, the transmission of desire from one subject to the other. This desire is always, already, a desire for something or for someone.

A Self That Is Created in the Heart of the Relation

I have always thought that what is conventionally called the "self" in psychology is a changing, unstable, malleable structure. This psychological way of interpreting the idea of a "self" is not obvious; it even seems to go against our basic intuition: we all think we are self-identical and perfectly autonomous. Nevertheless, when we are depressed or wracked with anguish, we no longer recognize ourselves. And when we fall in love, we are astonished with ourselves and say to ourselves, "It's impossible, I've become a different person." We are no longer the same; our self has become transformed. The memory that ties together these successive states, along with the forgetfulness that conceals from us the origin of our desires, apparently permits us to believe in the underlying continuity of a permanent identity. These factors organize in reality an ex post facto reconstruction that is completely illusory; the present self is always different from what it had been. It never ceases to create itself and recreate itself in the bosom of each relationship.

How can we understand such a rapidly moving sequence? Each of our desires, because it is a desire to be like the other, is, as we have seen, very mobile. It produces with each change of model a different psychological movement and thus a different self. Raymond Devos expresses this clearly:

"One often takes oneself for some one, when at bottom, one is several." We are indeed constantly being modified, kneaded, penetrated by otherness, led to detach ourselves from one model in order to adopt another, in whom we always believe we see a "surplus" of being that we lack. We also imitate our model despite ourselves, taking over from him everything we can: his appearance, his belongings, his desires, sometimes even his very being.

When a patient is in a hypnotic trance, this allows us to gain direct and easy access to his "unconscious"—from the point of view of mimetic psychology we would say, to the "otherness" of his desire—bypassing the habitual psychological roadblocks (forgetfulness, worldview, denial, and so on). In our mimetic perspective, hypnosis is especially interesting because it reveals and manifests a mechanism that operates in us without our noticing it: the imitation of the other's desire, the otherness that penetrates into us and works changes in us in every moment. Hypnosis thus reveals concretely how the self is constituted in the interdividual relation. It is the ultimate proof and illustration of mimetic desire. One might even call it "the distillation of mimetic desire," or a state of "pure mimetism." It shows the extent to which psychological movement comes from the other, the one I imitate. It is characterized by a modified state of consciousness, in which the patient submits himself entirely to the suggestions of the hypnotist, imitates his desire in a unidirectional manner, and undergoes a complete change in consciousness during the session.

Here, the interdividual relation becomes fixed in a single direction, from the suggesting hypnotist to the imitating patient, and this permits us to see and understand how the self becomes modified in the course of the exchange. The hypnotic relation is therefore very illuminating; it enables us to see quite clearly how the hypnotist's desire can produce through the hypnotic relation a new self in the patient, making his present self gradually dissolve while it makes him speak, act, and feel as the hypnotist wishes. And this new self engendered by the desire of the hypnotist appears with all the attributes of an "authentic" self: a new consciousness, a new memory, a new voice, a new motivation, and so on. What has happened? The hypnotic subject is as though magnetized: he models himself according to all the indications of the hypnotist, obeys his slightest injunction. The hypnotist thus manages, during the time of the session, to empty out the habitual desire that fashioned the self of the patient while substituting for it the hypnotist's own desire, thereby fashioning in him another self, and another consciousness. In the hypnotic rapport, the patient is able to recognize, though only for the moment, the mimetic origin of his desire.

The fact of hypnosis shows us that there is no self apart from desire, that it is desire that animates the self, and that the self is a "self-of-desire" or "desire-self." It is precisely because our consciousness is formed by otherness that it can be modified by and in the relation to the other the way it is in hypnosis. Otherwise hypnosis would be inexplicable and would seem like magic. On awakening, however, the hypnotic subject remembers nothing and immediately forgets that his desire was modeled on that of the hypnotist; he believes that he has remained unchanged. And if he goes on later to do something under the influence of a posthypnotic suggestion (such as to throw away his packet of cigarettes), he will believe once again that this action belongs to him and that he set it in motion himself. His prehypnotic illusion of autonomy and of the ownership of his desire remains intact.

This is why, with René Girard, I set aside the notion of an "individual," conceived as a self-contained and self-enclosed entity that can find the origin of its identity and freedom within itself. We have abandoned the "classical" psychology that describes that sort of self in favor of a new psychology of "interdividuality." As we conceive it, the true psychological reality is not situated within the individual but lies in the mysterious transparency of the relation between two persons. And this psychological relationship, this constant interaction, is entirely mimetic. It is characterized by the reciprocal movement of imitation and suggestion passing from one person to the other, a symmetrical movement that we forge and modify unceasingly. Our desire, and thus our self, forms in that "between," in that relation; the self is not something hidden away, sheltered, and fortified within itself, but the product of a continuous process of creation taking place at the crossroads of our encounters, within our abiding, symmetrical exchanges with those around us. It cannot be born except from these exchanges.

Because of the nature of our desire, which is always mimetic, to speak of an "authentic" self is really meaningless, at least if authenticity is supposed to refer to the capacity of a subject to determine all by itself what it desires without being influenced by others. From the point of view of a mimetic approach, the most "authentic" self would be one that recognizes the mimetic nature of its desire and thereby frees itself from the deceptive individualism that impedes understanding of oneself, of others, and of their relations.

When we are no longer subject to the illusion of the anteriority of our own desires—the idea, that is, that we desired whatever it is before the other did—when we misunderstand a little less the universal mimetic mechanisms that operate us, we arrive at a form of humility that consists of coming closer to ourselves and to the reality of our desire, and withdrawing a little from a too close proximity to the other. Because we are mimetic beings and will never be able to extricate ourselves from that reality, the apparent opacity of the self is made up of endless mirrorings. To fail to understand that fact prevents our desires from flowing freely in the midst of those multiple refractions, prevents us from opening ourselves without resistance to that ever-changing flow of life and of possibility. What really threatens us, what indicates our resistance to the flow of life, is the sudden immobility of our desire when it becomes fixated on a single model, a situation that condemns us to ever increasing rivalry and invites into us all the pathologies rivalry brings with it. The only way to become free from mimetism is to understand that we are always and totally immersed in it and that the rivalry that threatens us in every moment can be put at a distance only through the revelation of the mechanism that gives it birth.

A Self That Can Die and Be Reborn

When one considers one's life, one can observe in it a succession of selves that sometimes have no relation to one another. We are not necessarily the same as we were yesterday. We are not the same person with each other person. That can be seen most easily in the relations within a marriage. Caught up in the passion of love, the self becomes molded and transformed by the other's desire. That seems to be what we mean by "falling in love": a movement that turns us head over heels and transforms our very being without our even knowing what happened to us. A new self surges up who is no longer interested in what even yesterday held him and filled him. All his attention, his energy, his desires, his thoughts find themselves fixed upon one unique person. That is why young lovers feel as if they are the only ones in the world: nothing interests them any longer except being together.

This "birth" of a new self also has a cruel counterpart: if the self formed in the heart of the relationship finds itself abandoned, if it feels itself dropped by the beloved, it crumbles immediately, disappears, and dies. The death-anxiety that accompanies the fear of being abandoned is quite real. We feel an inner presentiment that the beloved, who feeds our desire, who makes us live with such fullness and intensity, could also, by disappearing, make us die. He or she will no longer communicate to us the desire that has formed our present self. This sense of being abandoned will give us a feeling of annihilation: "I no longer exist," "There's nothing left in me anymore," "If she has abandoned me, it's because I'm valueless," "I am nothing." And in fact, the self, needing to be completely reconstructed, will never be the same. It will have to find a new love if it is to take shape again. Such death-anxiety can disclose itself through many symptoms on the emotional level: distress, tears, anguish, insomnia, nightmares, hyperventilation, loss of appetite, diarrhea, and so on. And on the cortical level, in the form of paranoia, rationalization, a reconstructing of reality that goes on and on. Othello, in the grip of a tragic madness and overwhelming anguish, abandons himself to illusory jealousy and proceeds all the way to murder. This is also one of the reasons we never love two persons in exactly the same manner: the desire-self constructed within the relationship is different each time. If one is led to experience two or three great loves during one's lifetime, none will resemble the others despite their deep intensity—just as two hypnotists will each create a different self in the same patient.

It therefore seems to me necessary to supplement Girard's hypothesis about mimetic desire with three specifically psychological hypotheses:

- It is desire that engenders the self and by its movement brings the self to life.
- Desire is the origin of the self. The self is therefore in reality a self-of-desire. Another desire, the desire of another model, will bring with it the emergence of a different self, an-other-self-of-an-other-desire.
- A psychological reality is not situated in the tranquil opacity of anyone's "own body," contained in the reassuring totality of a "self," but rather in the mysterious transparency of the interdividual relation.

The Inseparability of Imitation and Suggestion

Before proceeding further, I must return to another essential fact of interdividual psychology: the rigorous correspondence between imitation and suggestion, those two vectors that constitute the "back and forth" of mimesis between two subjects and create through their ceaseless movement the interdividual relation.

From the point of view of this psychology, every relationship is made up of conjoined suggestions and imitations, because these two notions actually designate a single reality. Every imitation proceeds from a suggestion, and conversely, the imitation becomes itself a new suggestion that will be imitated in turn. If I copy the desire of another, it is because the other has suggested it to me, and my own expression of that desire will lead him to copy me himself.

Imitation and suggestion constitute therefore a single psychological reality, which itself is identical with the interdividual relation. They are mutually the cause and effect of each other, in identical proportions.

The oneness of imitation and suggestion as two identical vectors, but moving in contrary directions, can therefore be illustrated as follows:

Figure 1

One can say that subject A has suggested some gesture to subject B only if the latter has imitated it; conversely, every gesture of A that is reproduced, that is, imitated, by B will be seen as having been suggested to him by A. The linking of imitation and suggestion seems to me a significant contribution to the development of interdividual psychology. The importance accorded to suggestion by psychologists has always been immense. But strangely, very few have noticed and inquired into the inverse vector of suggestion, that is, imitation, which always correlates with suggestion immediately and with equal intensity. The classical psychology of the subject, which believes in the subject's autonomy, has always separated these two movements; the subject has been viewed as sometimes imitating the other, that is, undergoing influence from that other, and sometimes as suggesting a gesture or act or thought to the other and thereby exercising an influence on him. In the framework of interdividual psychology, on the contrary, these two terms can never be separated but are indissociable; the relationship between any two subjects is characterized systematically by a constant mutual influence. Every phenomenon of consciousness is in this sense a suggestion, and it finds its origin in the other.

The history of suggestion is closely tied up with the history of hypnosis. Freud himself set hypnosis aside as a therapy and replaced it with free association, a talking therapy in which the patient says whatever spontaneously comes to mind, in order to get around the process of self-censorship and enlarge the habitual field of consciousness. Freud designed psychoanalysis (in which the therapist, in contrast to the hypnotist, is never directive) to avoid the use of suggestion. He quickly realized that suggestion awakens a strong and fatal rivalry with the therapist, a rivalry that impedes healing. With the hypnotic method, a cure would be closely connected with the idea of a victory of the hypnotist over the "illness," and therefore over the patient too, since the latter can never be completely dissociated from his symptoms. During the hypnotic session, suggestion lies mainly on the side of the hypnotist and imitation on that of the patient. The hypnotic relation, while it lasts, is a completely peaceful affair; the patient simply yields to the hypnotist without putting up any resistance. Unfortunately, in many cases, when the hypnotic relation ends, the patient resents the hypnosis as an excessive and intrusive influence. He cannot accept the fact that another could impose his will on him to such an extent. He then quickly tries to turn the relation around and dominate the therapist by proving to him that he failed, showing him that the symptoms (and therefore the patient himself) are even stronger. Rivalry thus triumphs over healing.

Pierre Janet long ago identified that problem, which he called "somnambulistic passion"; once a hysteric has been hypnotized, he found, and the therapist has succeeded in making the symptoms disappear, they often come back a few days or a few weeks later.[7] When the hypnotic influence weakens, rivalry returns, bringing back the symptoms along with it in order to put the therapist in check. The patient forms a sort of alliance with his symptoms against the therapist, with no awareness of the mechanism that is coming back into play and preventing his healing. From then on, the hysteric will not leave the therapist alone, returning again and again to complain and to show him how defeated he is, and to try to influence him in turn: "Look, I'm still suffering. That's solid proof that you're worthless!"

To avoid this game of rivalry, this excessively close and intense connection between therapist and patient, Freud inaugurated another path. But it seems to me that the two vectors of which I have been speaking, imitation and suggestion, came back to trap him again later under the name of transference and countertransference, that is, the automatic and inevitable attachment of the patient to the analyst (in which the analyst embodies again various figures to whom the patient has been attached—replacing symbolically the patient's mother, a former lover, or a brother, and so on) and also the reciprocal attachment of the analyst to the patient. Such attachment, too, can turn negative and produce aggression. In the case of a positive transference, the patient wants to get better in response to the therapist's desire to heal, and thus to please him. In the opposite case, when the transference is negative, this will lead him to nurse distrust and hostility and to try to resist the cure so as to defeat his analyst.

I must add, finally, that the vectors of imitation and suggestion are animated by an incessant, rapid back-and-forth movement between A and B. This movement circulates in both directions. A imitates the suggestions of B while at the same time suggesting to B to imitate him in turn, and B does the same. Both influence and imitate each other simultaneously, so that ultimately no one can know who is copying whom.

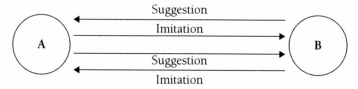

Figure 2

I have explained how the interdividual rapport of hypnosis is character-ized by the immobilizing of the two vectors: if A is the hypnotist, suggestion moves from A toward B, and imitation moves from B, the hypnotized, toward A. When this happens, one sees a new self appear in B, a somnambulistic self with new attributes: a different consciousness, a different memory, a different voice. This new self is an other-self-of-the-other-desire; the desire-self of A substituting for the desire-self of B, which is hypnotized, has swooned, is "asleep."

These rapid, multiple exchanges between A and B constitute the interdividual relation, with whatever affective tonality it may take on. In lovemaking, in an embrace, every caress from A suggests its reciprocal. B will respond with a caress for A. B's imitative response becomes a suggestion for A, who will respond in turn with another caress. Each imitation will at the same time be a suggestion. Conversely, in combat and conflict, in fisticuffs, every blow from A plays the role of a suggestion to B, whose counterblow is an imitation of A's violent gesture. But that imitation coming from B will also be a violent gesture that through suggestion will cause mounting aggression in A, and vice versa. One can see therefore that the mechanisms that feed either love or violence are really the same.

The discovery of mirror neurons, as we will see, confirms the nature and the meaning of these changes; this discovery shows that *the intention of a gesture* is already being imitated by the gesture's observer. The observer will then also be led to reproduce the action or the intention that he has observed, and in a manner that is both immediate and unavoidable. And the reproduction of the action will activate in turn the same mirror neurons in the one who observes it. Thus the intention of reaching out to take an apple will immediately produce its mirror image in the brain of the observer, and if he then stretches out his hand in turn to grasp it, as was suggested to him, he will trigger a similar neurological activity in those who see him do it. It is because certain of our neurons are triggered not only in performing an action but also in seeing it performed by another, or in perceiving that another intends to perform it, that we are constantly stimulated inwardly to reproduce and imitate the intentions and actions of those we observe. And thus we are able not only to understand the actions and intentions of another and to feel empathy, but also to imitate them, to learn, and to construct ourselves. It is precisely this "natural mimetism" that enables us to enter into contact with others. Autistic persons, who show greatly reduced activity in their mirror neurons, generally try to avoid all such contact, because they do not succeed in inwardly reproducing and understanding the actions of those around them and so are unable to enter into relationship with them.

Sometimes these exchanges take a less obvious form. In the presence of a person who manifests a desire for us, for example, we will not necessarily respond with a symmetrical desire for that other person. This is because to copy his or her desire *for us* means first of all for us to desire *ourselves*. That, indeed, is how we spontaneously respond: loving ourselves in imitation of the other's love for us, we feel flattered, and our self-esteem is comforted and reinforced. That configuration can be represented as a new form of triangulation: the aspiring lover (the subject), the beloved (the mediator), and the body of the beloved (the object). To imitate the other's desire means, in this case, to desire the same object, my body, and therefore to desire myself, which redoubles the desire of my lover, who imitates in turn the desire he stimulated in me.

In such a game of double mediation, the revelation of one's desire can arouse a desire that seems its opposite. It nonetheless arises from the same mimetic mechanism. This is what every successful seducer soon learns; he knows that to achieve his goal, he must mask his own desire and pretend indifference, set up false obstacles before the one he desires, make himself seem distant and unattainable; in brief, he must forbid himself to her.

The Sentiments: Colorations of the Mimetic Mechanism

Some have accused Girard, and me as well, of proposing a mechanistic, feelingless psychology, on the ground that mimesis and mimetic desire lack affective coloring. It seems to me, on the contrary, that the mimetic hypothesis analyzes

and brings to light elemental mechanisms that allow us to decode psychological and affective configurations in all their multiplicity and shimmering complexity, and this without in any way removing what makes them so dazzling.
Even if the game of cards as such remains always the same, no individual
game is the same as another. Each match remains unique and unpredictable,
conferring new pleasure, and will require a different analysis. We may know
the astronomical and mechanical principles that explain a sunset, but this will
in no way diminish or dissipate its splendor and magic. In fact, we will marvel
all the more by seeing how such simple and universal laws can offer us each
evening a spectacle so unique. Our emotional response suffers no disenchantment from understanding the mechanisms that give it birth.

Why should the mimetic theory, by laying bare the mechanisms of our
desires, necessarily weaken our sentiments? To understand how I fall in love
will not make me cease doing so, or diminish the refulgence of my emotions.
The revelation of mimetic desire will no doubt make me see that the desire
I experience for the one I love is not "essential," as I might be inclined to
believe. I will perhaps understand that the reason I have singled her out is
that another desired her before me, that it is he who pointed her out to me,
and that she is not as unique as I might like to think. Many pathologies of
couples come from the illusion of one member of the couple wanting to believe
absolutely in the uniqueness of the other. But I can still yield myself to that
delicious illusion and build a happy relationship with the other. This is why
I think our hypothesis is capable of bringing psychology into the domain of
science and extricating it from mythology. The mimetic principle is at the root
of all human relations, and even of the very possibility of those relations.

According to the mimetic principle, imitation is therefore the prime mover of
human relations. And its nature is profoundly ambivalent: it is wedded to a
universal mechanism from whose power no one can get loose and which is at
the origin of all relational dynamics, for better or for worse: love, generosity,
empathy, sympathy, and mutual aid, but also rivalry, jealousy, resentment,
violence, murder, and so on. It is imitation that permits relationships, and it is
also that which can undo them. Certainly love and desire will always be tinc-
tured with rivalry, and if there were no rivalry at all, we would be condemned
to pure love—a desire denuded of aggressive energy, which would only wish
us well, and which would deprive us of all the playful games of love, that is,
of all sexuality.

But that ambivalence, present as it may always be, must not become too
prominent. In a harmonious relationship, the part of rivalry must never gain

precedence over that of desire, lest it destroy it. Also, to maintain a relationship, especially if it is an amorous one, one must constantly protect it and relieve it of the covetous passions that desire can nourish. It is indeed a sad paradox that the same desire that unites us, that carries us toward another being, that can make our happiness, can also divide us and set us against each other, opening a fault line through which rivalry and jealousy can insinuate themselves, separate us from our beloved, and swiftly evict us from the paradise of love.

Is the genesis of desire concomitant with the genesis of humanity? That is what is taught us by one of the oldest texts of humanity, that of the first book of the Torah, which I would now like to comment on—less, though, as a religious text than as the subtlest and most perspicacious of psychological texts.

CHAPTER 2

The Creation and the Fall

I sometimes think that God, in creating man, rather overestimated His ability.

—*Oscar Wilde*

I would like to propose the hypothesis that the text of Genesis and the idea of "original sin" interpret through metaphor the birth of psychological man, that is, of humanity, of the couple, and of desire. In connection with this, I also propose to show that this birth of psychological man, like that of social man, is brought about by purely mimetic mechanisms.

"God Created Man in His Own Image"

Chapter 1 of Genesis, the first version of the creation story, sets the scene:

> In the beginning God created the heavens and the earth. Now the earth was
> a formless void, there was darkness over the deep, and God's spirit hovered
> over the water.[1]

The Creation is represented right from the start as a process of differentiation. The first thing created is difference. "Difference," wrote Gabriel Tarde in

Monadology and Sociology, "is the alpha and omega of the universe."[2] Genesis
1:3–10 tells the story of Creation and the establishing of stable differences:
light and darkness, earth and the seas.

On the third and fourth days, the process of differentiation continues
with the creation of plants and trees, the sun, the moon, and the stars.

On the fifth day, living beings are created. Perennial differences are established among them that will be transmitted from generation to generation:

> God created great sea-monsters and all the creatures that glide and teem in
> the waters in their own species, and winged birds *in their own species.* God
> saw that it was good. (Gen. 1:21)

I have added the emphasis on "in their own species" regarding the differentiation of the varieties of aquatic and winged beings; *species,* in Latin,
comes from the same root as *speculum,* the Latin word for "mirror." Those
beings are of the same species that can recognize each other by looking at
each other. Those are of the same species that we can recognize by looking at
them, because they resemble each other in the midst of all the differences that
constitute their specificity. The differentiation of species is assured by reproduction, which is the mechanism through which their difference becomes
perpetuated in the identity and continuity of each species.

Verse 25 goes on to talk about the differences among animals:

> God made wild animals in their own species, and cattle in theirs, and every
> creature that crawls along the earth in its own species.

The Creation began with the organization of mineral differences, which
are changeless, then vegetable and animal differences, which are perennial
because they are reproducible. Reproduction guarantees both difference and
identity simultaneously, and it also guarantees the succession of generations.
In the mechanism of reproduction we see the genetic dimension of mimesis,
to which I will return in a moment.

The creation of man is radically distinct from all those creations that came
before it:

> God said, "Let us make man in our own image, in the likeness of ourselves,
> and let them be masters of the fish of the sea, the birds of heaven, the cattle,
> all the wild beasts and all the reptiles that crawl upon the earth."

God created man in the image of himself, in the image of God he
created him, male and female he created them. (Gen. 1:26–27)

The terms "image" and "likeness" suggest a physical similitude. They
recall the "mirroring" similitude in animals implied by the term "species"
(from *speculum*) when it was said that God created them each according to its
species (*selon leur espèce*). Would God, man, and woman then be of the same
kind? If so, they would be able to recognize each other. Also, in creating man
"in His own image," God differentiates man radically from all the animals
created before him and confers on him power and dominion over them:

God blessed them, saying to them, "Be fruitful, multiply, fill the earth and
subdue it. Be masters of the fish of the sea, the birds of heaven and all the
living creatures that move on earth." (Gen. 1:28)

Paul Ricoeur comments on this from the point of view of a philosopher
and moralist:

The *imago dei*—there we have both our being-created and our innocence;
for the "goodness" of the creation is no other than its status as "creature."
All creation is good, and the goodness that belongs to man is his being
the image of God. Seen retrospectively, from the point of view of sin, as a
"prior" state in mythical language, the likeness appears as an absence of
guilt, as innocence; but his goodness is altogether positive; it is sin that is
the nothingness of vanity.[3]

Some might object that the story of Adam and Eve is mythic, but in a
time before the development of scientific method, myth could be the precise
expression of intuitions that science is only now catching up with. As Paul
Ricoeur put it, perhaps we should not say, "'The story of the 'fall' is *only* a
myth'—that is to say, something less than history—but, 'The story of the
fall has the greatness of myth'—that is to say, has more meaning than a true
history. But what meaning?"[4] From our own point of view, by emphasizing
that man is created in the image and likeness of God, the myth brings clearly
to light the fact that the spatial dimension of mimesis is inscribed in man's
being. The creation of man is presented not as a fabrication, a construction,
a work, or an act of will, as in the case of the preceding acts of creation, but
rather as a mimetic process, a mimetic transfer of information from God to
His creature made in His image. The Biblical myth points to the mimetic

specificity of the human species, and to the inscription of mimetism and imitation in human nature from the moment of its creation. The mimetic theory finally brings scientific clarity to what the myth perceived confusedly. I will try to show this by following the Biblical text verse by verse.

At the beginning of the Creation, the spatial dimension of mimesis, which molds this new creature, has to do only with appearance, with form. In this I see the first condition of man, as a newborn coming to life in full innocence. Josy Eisenberg suggests this possible way of reading the story:

> The story of Creation is so rich in symbols that one can read it entirely on the symbolic level. The garden would not be a place, but a situation: the first condition of man. So also, Adam would not be a man but rather the archetype of humanity.[5]

I emphasize the inscription of the spatial dimension of imitation in each human being, from the moment of creation, and it is that inscription that differentiates man in the Biblical narrative from all other animals. Aristotle said the same thing: "Imitation is natural to man from childhood, one of his advantages over the lower animals being this, that he is the most imitative creature in the world, and learns at first by imitation."[6]

A being who is capable of imitating one like him is no longer strictly and exclusively subject to the genetic dimension of universal mimesis, which reproduces the same schemes of behavior and the same reactions from generation to generation. This human mimetic capacity, because it is specifically cultural, confers on man his liberty: he is able to imitate other men, and he is able to imitate God. It is this, implicit in his creation, that makes man radically different from all other beings.

In his first beginnings, as a newborn child, man exercises his capacity for imitation only in relation to form or appearance. As we saw earlier, the other modes of mimesis, those bearing on having, on being, and on desire, are never far away; it is precisely that further mimesis that leads to man's exit from paradise.

This affinity between God and human beings at the very origin of the process of creation seems to me to constitute an invitation to participate in the creative process. The new dimension of mimesis that appears with the creation of man frees him from genetic necessity and renders him free and capable of learning new things through imitation. This new aptitude makes it possible for him to share in the work of creation, to become a co-creator with his creator.

God, having manifested his creativity for five days, seems on the sixth to give that creative capacity to the man whom he has just made "in his image." Consider an animal: it is a finished being, perfect "according to its species," and it will never become anything other than simply what it is. Man, on the other hand, appears as an unfinished being, but free, endowed with the capacity for imitation and able to complete his creation by going on to create himself. Man is the only being capable of recreating the world and his environment by recreating nature through art—and to share in the process of his own creation. Man is a creature in a constant state of becoming, one who has a story of his own. Is he the actor or the spectator of his own story? To just what extent does his becoming depend on his own will? And is that will free? All of these questions that have stimulated philosophical and theological debates for centuries have their origin in these first few verses of the Bible.

Something the Biblical text does not say explicitly, but which is implicit in all the dialogues among the four personages of that story, is that language constitutes the other specific characteristic of man. A human being, reproduced by the genetic dimension of mimesis, is given freedom by the spatial dimension of mimesis, which makes him capable of copying a form or a gesture in space and therefore of appropriating knowledge and new techniques, something for which animals, governed as they are by predetermined schemes of behavior, have little capacity. Man is also capable of copying a sound and reproducing it, bringing it to voice again. Repetition, the temporal dimension of mimesis, in constituting memory, completes man's capacities and enables him to be the enactor of his own story.

"He breathed into his nostrils a breath of life . . ."

The second story of creation has a proliferating wealth of symbols. A second account of the creation of man completes the first:

> Yahweh God shaped man from the soil of the ground and blew the breath of life into his nostrils, and man became a living being. (Gen. 2:7)

In the psychological perspective that I advocate, this text seems to me to indicate that the self is pervaded with otherness. God molds clay from the earth and animates it with "a breath of life": the self is fashioned by the Other that he copies, that he imitates, and it is the Other who breathes into him life, movement, which is to say in psychological terms, desire. To conceive of psychological movement within a closed, "monadic" subject would be an illusion.

It is the Other's desire that creates desire within the self, through suggestion. The self's desire copies and models itself on the Other's desire by imitating it. The self and the Other are interchangeable, indissociable; that is, they are constantly in interaction because of their reciprocal porosity, a porosity that characterizes the mimetic relation as such. The movement of either one is communicated to the other and vice versa, in a constant to and fro: first one will imitate a model, but from the very fact of that imitation, the model will begin to imitate his imitator in turn, with his own desire being given new life by that game of mirrors. The imitator will become the model's model, and the model will become the imitator of the one who imitates him.

The text of Genesis contains many more surprising elements that reinforce this hypothesis. The otherness of God is not the otherness of man. The myth sets us on the path of psychological discovery. God is not my *alter ego* in the way that other human beings are. This Other who fashions me can, if our relationship avoids rivalry, make of me an image of God. Mimetic escalation is not necessarily something fatal: it can also be the way one hears the call of paradise.

Let us continue with our reading:

> Yahweh God planted a garden in Eden, which is in the east, and there he put
> the man he had fashioned. (Gen. 2:8)

> Then Yahweh God gave the man this command, "You are free to eat of all the
> trees in the garden. But of the tree of the knowledge of good and evil you are
> not to eat; for, the day you eat of that, you are doomed to die." (Gen. 2:16)

God puts the man in the garden at the risk of his eating from that tree. While doing so, he calls the attention of the man to the tree, singles it out from among all the other trees in the garden. He creates a new difference, one that does not correspond to any appearance: this tree is distinguished only by the danger that is involved in eating it. But this difference is fundamental: it completes the creation of man by conferring liberty on him. He is warned and put on his guard, but he is nonetheless free to choose. And his choice, as we will see, is decisive: it is the choice between life and death, of his remaining in the garden and in innocence, or his entering into an unknown world. This liberty truly brings to a finish the creation that is the work of God.

The serpent will soon exploit the uniqueness of that tree and will transform what was a warning, a counsel, a prophecy, into a prohibition, and in doing so he will pervert the gaze of the creature who listens to him.

What is also noteworthy is that the tree is designated neither by name nor by its fruit but by the fact that it will confer "knowledge of good and evil." It is this knowledge that God designates as a toxic difference and the cause of the death that will come from this tree.

What is the "knowledge of good and evil"? It is not a form of objective knowledge or knowledge of how to do something: Adam knows his way around his world perfectly; the garden is his domain, and it is he who, in verses 19 and 20, gives names to all the animals that God parades before him.[7] Nor is that knowledge a form of moral discernment or a capacity for judgment: Adam already has that, otherwise God's counsel or warning would convey no meaning to him.

According to the tradition of Saint Augustine and Saint Thomas Aquinas, the "knowledge of good and evil" has to do with a claim to moral autonomy: to eat of the fruit of this tree is to appropriate the knowing of good and evil to oneself, to set oneself up as the judge of what is good and what is evil. It is therefore an attempt to overturn the divine order.

That is one interesting way to read it. Even more interesting from my point of view is that suggested in the commentary of Josy Eisenberg:

> This tree is the place where Good and Evil are confused together. To speak of fusion is to speak also of confusion . . . this is the new situation with which Adam is confronted: there exists a tree—a world—where Good and Evil are in a mixed state.[8]

And further on, Eisenberg adds:

> The mixture of Good and Evil in all things is itself, according to Jewish mysticism, the dominant characteristic of the human story.[9]

Developing this idea, I propose to show that if the forbidden tree gives rise to desire, it is mimetic desire that makes good and evil spring from this prohibition and, with them, all the relative, subjective, and generative differences of rivalry.

"This is to be called woman, for this was taken from man."

After having created the differences that are stable and immutable, then the perennial differences of genetic continuity, and finally what one may call the "moral" difference between fidelity (imitation of God as a model) and

disobedience, God gives Adam a companion. If the otherness of God in relation to Adam might be spoken of as "vertical," that of the woman God creates
for him is a "horizontal" otherness.

> Yahweh God said, "It is not right that the man should be alone. I shall make
> him a helper." (Gen. 2:18)

Here the French translation of André Chouraqui clarifies the meaning
further; it modifies the notion of the help the woman would bring as a help-
mate by using the word *contre,* which makes her an equal, a challenger:

> It is not good for the one of earth to be alone! I will make for him an aid
> opposite [*contre*] him.[10]

Or one might say, the woman is for the man "an aid opposing him."

This is an admirable lesson in psychology, a formula that would have
fascinated Sacha Guitry.[11] Indeed, what was lacking for the creation of psychological man was an *alter ego.* If God did not create such an *alter ego,* "in
the face of" or "opposite" the man, there would have been no possibility of
dialectic, of psychological movement, that is, of desire.

And so God created woman. Here the translation by Chouraqui seems
particularly rich:

> YHVH (Adonai) Elohim makes a torpor to fall on the one of earth. He sleeps.
> He takes one of his ribs and encloses it with flesh.
> YHVH (Adonai) Elohim makes the rib that he took from the one of earth
> into a woman.
> He makes her come toward the one of earth.
>
> The one of earth says:
>
> "This one, this time, she is the bone of my bones, the flesh of my flesh,
> she will be called 'woman'—*Isha:*
> yes, from man—Ish—she has been taken." (Gen 2:21–23)

Let us note that God creates a companion for man and gives her to him.
Adam immediately loves her and cries out: "Isha." He conforms himself
mimetically to the choice that God has made for him in giving him this gift.
In this transcendent, vertical relation, God gives and man receives. That is not

all: God *has* and man *takes,* as will also soon be the case at the foot of the tree. In the transcendent relationship there is no place for any form of rivalry. But that will not be the case in the reciprocal, horizontal relationship.

In its characteristically redundant way, the Bible insists again on the identity of self and other. The self is always "an other," pervaded by otherness. The story of the creation of man had already emphasized this. That of the woman further confirms it.

But why a rib? On this point Eisenberg's analysis seems to me particularly pertinent:

> We wonder if Adam was really alone in his first situation. According to the common reading of the text of Genesis, it would seem that God created man as a male at first and that he then brought the woman into being by drawing her from that man's rib. But that reading seems debatable if one remembers that the creation of Adam was presented in the Bible as being simultaneously that of a male and a female:
>
> > "Elohim created the Adam in his image,
> > in the image of Elohim created He him,
> > male and female He created them." (Gen. 1:27)
>
> Therefore many Jewish exegeses suggest a quite different reading of the story of the creation of man. This is notably the case with the *Zohar.* What does that text say? . . . Essentially that the Adam was created *double.* Adam was androgynous; nevertheless, the counterpart desired by God—an "aid opposite him [*une aide en face*]"—did not yet exist, because the two androgynous parts had their backs turned to each other, rather like Siamese twins.
>
> God then separated the two parts of the androgynous one. Pursuing the line of interpretation developed in the commentaries, one might say they suggest reading the text not as:
>
> > "He took one of his ribs."
> > But as:
> > "He took one of his sides."[12]

The *Zohar's* reading certainly wins our own approval. It also connects this myth with the famous myth of Aristophanes in Plato's *Symposium,* which speaks of how in the beginning there were three types: the male made up of a double man, the female made up of a double woman, and the androgyne made up of a man and a woman. After they had rebelled against the gods, Zeus cut them in two and set them in front of each other, while turning their faces to look at the cut in order to teach them some humility. Plato, too, needed to create *doubles,* in order to explain psychological movement, that is, desire: from now on, each half would feel a *lack,* the lack of his lost half, and that lack would be what we call desire. In Genesis, as in Plato, desire cannot come into being apart from otherness, and in both sources, desire, which is the very essence of the human, is like a factory defect that man bears with him from his beginning, from the time of his fall into the world, that is, from his birth.

The Absence of Shame

Let us return to the Book of Genesis. The Creation is now finished. The man and the woman are both present in the Garden of Eden, and both are complete: they can eat, drink, sleep, copulate, and walk around. Everything is marvelous and freely available. And yet, psychologically speaking, nothing is happening. Certainly the man has intelligence: he is superior to the animals; it is he who names them, and he fully recognizes that the woman is identical with him, his *alter ego.* But there is no psychological movement, no desire. The text says this clearly:

> Now, both of them were naked, the man and his wife, but they felt no shame before each other. (Gen. 2:25)

In sum, they see no difference between them.

The power of the Biblical account is clearly seen here: God separates the man from the woman, distinguishes between them, individualizes a part, a "side" of the man, in order to make the woman. But at this stage, the man and woman are still indifferent regarding their difference; it poses no problem to them: "They felt no shame in front of each other." God's creation is not the sword of Zeus brutally cleaving the original androgyne. The splitting in the Greek myth is not a divine creation; it is a brutal rupture that divides man and woman, the two halves of the androgyne.

Thus God created the woman by separating her from the man, by individualizing that part of Adam that will from now on be his otherness. In the Biblical story, it is rather the serpent who will play the role of the sword of Zeus in dividing first the woman from God and then the woman from the man.

The absence of desire is manifest "clinically," one might say, by the absence of shame. Shame—or sexual modesty—is one of the ingredients of eroticism. Erotic desire is the ultimate example of the "mixing" of good and evil, positive and negative, attraction and repulsion, tenderness and violence. Desire, which is quintessentially a mixture of two opposites, is absent from paradise for the moment, and it is this absence that is signified by the absence of "shame" before nakedness.

In contrast to the myth of Aristophanes in Plato, the Bible is not satisfied with this lack, with the simple separation of the androgyne into its two halves, the simple creation of sexual difference and otherness, as an explanation for the genesis of desire. At this point in the Biblical story, all the elements are in place and still *desire has not yet made its appearance.* The appetites, needs, and instincts of the man and woman are completely satisfied. And yet, psychology and psychological movement do not exist: in that Eden where the creatures are in every way satisfied, contented, and filled to the brim, nothing is happening. "Happy people have no history," as Tolstoy said. The conditions necessary for the appearance of desire are present, but they are not sufficient for it.

It is at this point in the story that the Bible gives us a great lesson in psychology: it will show us in the third chapter how psychology, history, and desire are born together. And this will be clearly a matter of mimetic desire.

The Serpent, the Symbol of Mimetic Desire

Chapter 3 opens with the appearance of the serpent:

> Now, the snake was the most subtle of all the wild animals that Yahweh God had made. (Gen. 3:1)

The subtlest, the most mischievous—that formula has had a future; in the Catholic tradition the serpent has always been interpreted as Mischief itself, Evil, the Demon, the Devil, the Tempter. But this serpent is an allegorical figure. What psychological reality does he represent? André Chouraqui, who translates Genesis 3:1 as follows, suggests a clue:

> The serpent was naked,[13] more than any living beast of the field that Yahveh Elohim had made . . .

As we saw above, Chapter 2 had ended with:

> Now both of them were naked, the man and his wife, but they felt no shame in front of each other.

And Chapter 3 begins with the description of the serpent as the most naked of all the animals created by God.

Before the Fall, the man and woman were naked, certainly, but no desire had begun to intrude itself into their need for each other; they are described as "one flesh" (2:24). After the Fall, Adam and Eve discovered that they were naked, experienced embarrassment, and "sewed fig-leaves together to make themselves loin-cloths." (3:7)

Thus nakedness after the Fall represents desire. But not desire in the mere sense of sexual desire, which we habitually confuse more or less with instinct, drive, or physical attraction. Rather, it is a matter, as I will try to show, of mimetic desire, which infiltrates human relations and bends or perverts our instincts, needs, and drives. The serpent, more "naked" than all living creatures, is the symbol of mimetic desire, as his action will demonstrate.

The presence of the serpent in this story raises questions. Paul Ricoeur underscores this: "Why was the origin of evil *not* restricted to Adam? Why was an extraneous figure retained and introduced?"[14] Ricoeur sketches a reply:

> In the figure of the serpent, the Yahwist may have been dramatizing an important aspect of the experience of temptation—the experience of quasi-externality. Temptation would be a sort of seduction from without; it would develop into compliance with the apparition which lays siege to the "heart"; and, finally, to sin would be to *yield*. . . . The serpent, then, represents this passive aspect of temptation, hovering on the border of the outer and the inner; the Decalogue calls it "covetousness" (Tenth Commandment).[15]

Now, that "covetousness" of which the tenth commandment speaks has on a number of occasions been identified by René Girard as mimetic desire.[16]

In my view, the serpent is an allegorical representation of mimetic desire. For one thing, he is described as the most "naked" of living creatures. And this "most" that characterizes his nakedness—it is precisely this that is remarked on at a time when the nakedness of Adam and Eve still remains, for the moment, unnoticed and indifferent, simply natural to them. The serpent's surplus of nakedness announces, therefore, an already present cultural element in addition to the natural, an addition that hints to us that this nudity is capable of awakening "covetousness," that is, mimetic desire.

Furthermore, the serpent injects his venom into the heel of the human being. This is a characteristic of mimetic desire: the poisoning that ensues represents the transfer of desire from one subject to another, the contamination of one by the desire of another. This is an allegorical symbolism one comes across frequently; it is especially exemplified by tarantulism.[17] How can we confirm the hypothesis that the serpent is an allegory of mimetic desire? To do that, we must examine the text closely.

At the beginning of chapter 2 of Genesis, the man and the woman are happy, they constitute one flesh; they are naked before each other, but they experience no shame with regard to that, no more than do animals have any sense of being naked. Nothing separates them; their nudity is not a difference that distinguishes them or embarrasses them. It simply doesn't matter, since they are united. Then the mimetic nudity, envious and rivalrous, of the serpent begins to worm its way in.

Budding Loves

Let us try for a moment to imagine, and to talk about in language closer to that of our own time, what the life of this couple might have been like before the intrusion of the serpent and therefore of the mimetic rivalry that will separate them. All stories of couples begin in something like this way:

Evening falls over the garden. The last rays of the sun gently color the plain and are reflected in the stream at the edge of which they are sitting. Adam turns toward Eve and says:

"You are the woman of my life, the only one, unique. I've loved you from the moment I saw you."

"I feel the same. Your presence fills me with happiness."

"It is because we belong to one another and we form a single soul that God has made time empty: our love lives in the instant and is eternal."

Arm in arm, Adam and Eve rise to go home. Adam continues:

"I have to tell you that the other day, when you went off to gather fruit, I felt as if I were lost, as if part of me had suddenly been amputated. I tried in vain to distract myself. But your absence was unbearable. It was more present to me than all the presences that surrounded me."

"I love what you are telling me. Swear to me that you'll never love anyone else."

"I could never do anything except love you forever—and you?"

"I think about you and dream about you all the time. It seems to me that this enchantment increases and grows stronger each day. I love to wake up next to you, and I love to fall asleep in your arms. Without you, life would have no meaning."

Thus one might imagine the conversation in the Garden of Eden. Up to this point, this is an allegory representing all budding loves: each of the lovers feels the other was created for him or for her and is a part of himself or herself—with the one enormous difference that all the budding loves we can experience or observe now unfold in the world of desire, after the Fall. It is in this alone, this feeling of being made for each other, that every budding love that wants to be unique, pure, and absolute resembles that of Adam and Eve. In our own world, such love will necessarily, through the mimetic and ambivalent nature of desire, become colored with rivalry and lose its purity by letting itself be contaminated by murkier sentiments: wanting to possess the other, to dominate the other, to be jealous of the other, or to turn away from the other precisely because we possess him or her. The happy fullness of those first hours will thus yield and generally give way to confusion and discord.

In his book *I Love You: Everything about Amorous Passion,* Francesco Alberoni describes this as "the birth state" of love.[18] For Alberoni, twenty necessary criteria must be found together for one to be able to talk about true love. I will summarize only the most essential of these:

- The loved one is unique. Each elicits the full attention and preoccupation of the other. The lovers feel themselves to be the only people alive, and they experience a feeling of liberation and of revelation in a transfigured world.
- Love gives a new meaning to life and to the world. This sense of meaning produces in each of the partners enormous energy, in a multiplying effect. Life is given meaning by their relationship, which takes on a sacred character and casts a veil over all other relationships.
- Love develops within the alliance they form, in their complicity; the loved one takes priority over everything else. His or her faults fade away; he or she possesses all excellences. Those who criticize the loved one are unjust. This alliance and complicity take concrete form in a project that consolidates the couple. It is this project—whatever it may be—that maintains their unity and structures the time of the couple; modest or grandiose, limited or global, secret or open, the project justifies the couple.

That being said, *love needs care.* The Greeks represented love in their mythology with the traits of a pudgy-cheeked baby: Eros. Love, like such a child, needs care and attention to grow and develop. A love that is neglected or ill cared for, like an abandoned child, withers and dies. One must nurture a love in order that it may flourish, as one must love a child so that it will grow.

When lovers discover their love, they feel a sense of wonder before each other and before everything that goes on within them and between them.

This sense of a miracle that is taking place and in which one participates leads to a moment of thankful prayer and makes the lovers seek from each other a commitment to perpetuate that state—even though it has come to them as a gift, something they have had nothing to do with causing. They would like to be able to prolong by an act of will the grace they have received, to master the miracle in order to perpetuate it. Similarly, it feels to lovers as if they are the only ones in the world, that time is abolished for them (just as in the Garden of Eden, time did not yet exist). Their being together brings an illusion of eternity. Any separation is unbearable to them: "You miss one being alone, and the whole world is empty." Adam, without Eve, felt as if he had suffered an amputation!

In the framework of mimetic psychology, it is the interdividual relation that engenders by its movement what, in each subject, can be called the self. It must be admitted, then, that it is not the encounter of two selves that creates the relation, but rather the relation that gives birth to each of the selves.

Love is this relation that creates in each of the lovers a new self, which is the *self-of-desire of the other.* Every separation, every abandonment, therefore, creates a death agony, because the self-of-desire, if it is not sustained and maintained by the desire of the other, risks really dissolving and disappearing: Mme. de Tourvel, abandoned by Valmont, dies because she has no existence outside that interdividual relation.

Love is at its birth, then, total, fusional, miraculous; one could even call it paradisal. That fusional state recalls the one that existed before the forbidden fruit, that is, before our entry into time. The text of Genesis depicts a mythic state of being that human beings must never, in principle, be able to experience. And yet many of them have a strong feeling of living in that state, and it transports them to a garden outside of time where they are the only ones and where they form, as two alone together, the totality of the world. Waking up from this dream can be painful. Some couples succeed in sustaining that initial sense of marvel throughout their lives; for others, on the other hand, it can degenerate into a veritable pathology of fusion: for not having known how to establish the relationship on a sound footing, their closeness condemns them to a losing quest for endless romantic excitement—or to rivalry.

The Exit from the Paradise of Love

In most cases, just as in Genesis, the lovers will leave the garden to enter into the world of complexity, will leave the dream to enter real life, leave eternity to enter time.

One day Eve returned from her gathering with a distracted look that Adam had never seen in her. He immediately felt anxious and said:

"My love, what happened to you? Are you worried about something?"

"No, everything's fine, leave me alone . . ."

In the face of this response, something without precedent in his life, he remains silent. A feeling of emptiness comes over him. He feels himself abruptly shut out from his companion's thinking and from her world. None of this makes any sense to him, and he experiences unknown and painful emotions. All of a sudden it begins to feel too warm. He feels as if he is suffocating, he starts to sweat, tries to hide in the shadows, then he swoons and loses consciousness. A few moments later he comes to; she is wiping his face with cool water. She smiles when he opens his eyes, and the world quickly recovers its stability.

"What happened to me?"

"You stayed in the sun too long!"

"No, I remember, I felt a great emptiness when you refused to answer me. I beg you, tell me what happened to you today."

"You won't get angry?"

"On the contrary, if you don't tell me, I'll never be the same."

"I met a strange being at the bottom of the garden."

Adam remains speechless. A strange being? He thought they were all alone here. Finally, he murmurs, "What being?"

"Oh, some creature[19] who doesn't resemble you at all. But he's intelligent and clever; he makes interesting conversation."

This news, of course, leaves Adam feeling "stupid." He doesn't understand. How could Eve become interested in another creature? Isn't he all she needs anymore? He feels an immense anxiety, but he wants to know: "Who is this?"

"His name is Serpent. He pointed out something really strange: there is one tree in the middle of the garden whose fruit God has forbidden us to eat."

Adam feels a bit reassured and recovers his voice: "What does that matter? There are hundreds of trees in the garden bearing delicious fruit. Why should we need something God has forbidden us?"

"But why did he forbid it? Did you ever ask him?"

"My love, I'm not interested in anything but you. You possess all the trees and all the fruits in the garden, and I belong to you. What importance could that tree have for me? It's nothing extraordinary!"

"That's not what the Serpent thinks!"

Adam is perplexed. He looks at the tree with a new sort of attention, but he can't find anything special about it. He wonders what the Serpent could have said to

Eve to make her see something that doesn't exist. Who, then, is this Serpent, and where does he come from? Why did God make that creature, who comes and worms his way between the perfect creatures that he made in his own image? A surge of anger rises up in him against God, which he immediately represses: "What's coming over me? I'm losing my head, I'm lost." He calls Eve, Eve his love, whose words have driven him mad, but from whom a word or a caress would bring him peace: "Explain it to me, Eve."

"The Serpent knows for certain that if we eat of the fruit of that tree, we won't die but rather we would become like God, divine beings, knowing good and evil."

"What does that knowledge matter to us? God has given us everything. He gave me life, and he gave me Eve. There's nothing else I need. Let's forget about all that."

"You have no imagination or ambition! I'm disappointed in you. I thought you loved me . . ."

"I love you, and we are one flesh, but I don't want you going away from me, and I don't want you to talk to that Serpent any more."

"The Serpent knows a lot. Come with me, let's eat some of that fruit and become gods."

Adam detests himself for not being able to say "No!"

A Desire That Separates

That is one possible way to read Genesis: the couple is formed, and it has the impression of recovering its unity. The man and woman have been created, before our very eyes, for each other, and also from each other. That's what budding love is like: the feeling of having recovered one's other half, of becoming one with her. This is a state of fusion, which eclipses everything in the world, all differences, conflicts, and rivalries, which sums up within itself all of one's previously scattered desires, making both models and rivals fade from view.

This situation is mythic, and therefore unstable and ephemeral, but for as long as it lasts, the two halves of the androgyne find each other again, recognize themselves, and are cemented together: each fills the other completely, healing the horrible cut left by the sword of Zeus, the wound in the one spouse identical with the wound in the other. Their reunion seems miraculous and at the same time inevitable, inscribed, it seems, for all eternity with the words, "You were destined for me."

In this state, the lovers are alone in the world, in the Garden of Eden. They are in paradise and live in the instant, that is, in eternity, outside of time.

What will cause the catastrophe? In the text of Genesis, it is the intervention of a third party who will make the couple leave paradise and enter the world and time. Not in this case the banal rival of ordinary stories, but an allegorical third one who is always there, a third who slithers between them, who insinuates himself into their midst, who separates and divides them from one another, who hurls them into the real world but at the same time clothes them with the fullness of their humanity.

This third who forms their humanness, who constitutes their psychological and anthropological reality is mimetic desire, rivalrous desire. But the Biblical text is much less mythic than that of Plato. The violence of the sword that severs the halves in Plato's myth is replaced here by a major psychological lesson: it is the serpent, the allegorical representation of covetousness and therefore of mimetic desire that insinuates itself between the man and the woman and between man and God, separating and dividing them and making Adam and Eve enter into rivalry, that is, into the world. Fusion already contains, therefore, the seed of separation: each extreme summons the other—that is, the oscillation between radical absence and absolute presence annuls the distance that alone could make connection between the two of them possible.

Let us observe how mimetic desire invites the two lovers to approach the forbidden tree:

> [The serpent] asked the woman, "Did God really say you were not to eat from any of the trees in the garden? (Gen. 3:1)

In order to induce a resisting subject into hypnosis, Milton Erickson advises one to pose only questions that will elicit negative answers: "Are you cold?—No—Are you hot?—No—Is the chair uncomfortable?—No." When the capacity for negation has been exhausted by this sequence, Erickson begins to introduce his suggestion: "Are you beginning to feel relaxed? . . ."—"Yes," says the subject, after feeling pretty much finished with the "No"s. The serpent uses the same sort of technique to introduce his own suggestion:

"So God said that *all* the trees in the garden were forbidden to you?" "No, certainly not," answers the woman and feels reassured. Her distrust is anesthetized because she has been able to correct what the apparently naive and ill-informed animal has been saying. Gently she explains to him:

"We may eat the fruit of the trees in the garden. But of the fruit of the tree in the middle of the garden God said, 'You must not eat it, nor touch it, under pain of death.'" (Gen. 3:2–3)

At this stage of the story, a new psychologically fundamental, intellectual mechanism has just been introduced into the human spirit: *comparison*. The comparison suggested to Eve by the serpent enters into her perception of that tree and of all the others. From that comparison, as always, difference arises: the difference between that tree and the others is established by the prohibition.

Josy Eisenberg points out that God never forbade them to touch that tree, but only to eat its fruit.[20] Eve's confusion about this is a sign that she is beginning to be hooked, to become responsive to the serpent's power of suggestion; her attention has become focused on the comparison, the difference, and the prohibition, all of which are mimetic mechanisms. The proof of this is that she experiences and resents that prohibition "as a stronger one than it really is."[21] It is precisely this that the serpent wants: to draw the attention of the woman to the supposedly enormous *difference* between that tree and all the others, and by doing so to endow it with a magnetic force that will attract her appropriative mimesis toward it. He obviously cannot accomplish that by way of any real need, appetite, or instinct. The only way to produce such a psychological movement in a being so happy, satisfied, and fulfilled is to bring mimetic mechanisms into play. The serpent, this clever being who "knows already" and has long ago ceased to be innocent, who is already "naked," already in the world, the adult world, thus awakens mimetic desire in Eve: "The model, God, has given you everything. But he has kept one tree for himself. There is the difference. There is the obstacle. There is the prohibition. There, therefore, is the desirable!"

Eve is not yet convinced. She weighs in the balance this particularly designated *having* and the threat of death that God spoke of. The model always seems to be terribly protective of what he has. The prohibition whips up desire, but the threatened danger, real or supposed, is often dissuasive.

The serpent knows all this better than we do. So he first sets about appeasing these fears:

Then the serpent said to the woman, "No! You will not die!" (Gen. 3:4)

To calm her fear is important, but to stimulate psychological movement, the serpent brings her mimesis to a focus not on the having, but on the *being* of the model:

"God knows in fact that on the day you eat it your eyes will be opened and you will be like gods, knowing good from evil." (Gen. 3:5)

The slide from the *having* of the model toward his *being* is here represented by three elements:

- The fact that the having is of little importance.
- The absence of the need for any effort or struggle to take possession of what the model has. All she needs to do is just reach out her hand and take it. The model, God, will not *react* to the gesture of appropriation; he will simply allow its consequences to unfold.
- Finally, and most importantly, the ontological consequences that will follow from the transgression have no relation to the object.

The appropriation of the object only guides one toward the appropriation of the model's being; it symbolizes the desire to appropriate and incorporate his being, his power. With this, we pass from mimetic desire to metaphysical desire.

The Transfiguration of the Object under the Influence of Desire

What appropriative mimesis could not trigger, metaphysical desire has obtained: from now on this desire, purely mimetic as it is, aims beyond the object at the very being of the one on whom that object confers a *knowledge* and *power* that he is trying to hold out of reach. The first effect of mimetic rivalry is the transfiguration of the object; it becomes an *object of desire*:

> The woman saw that the tree was good to eat and pleasing to the eye, and that it was enticing for the wisdom that it could give. (Gen. 3:6)[22]

Eve sees that tree in a whole new way: she sees it as a distinct object because someone has designated it as different and forbidden. Mimetic desire has brought to view features that were previously invisible. It has transfigured the object into the content of what Girard and I call a "hallucinatory psychosis of desire."

André Chouraqui's translation seems to bring out more clearly the idea that mimetic desire makes her see the object of desire differently:

> The woman sees that the tree is good to eat, yes, appetizing to the eyes, covetable, this tree, because it can make one perspicacious.

This translation shows the metamorphosis of the object under the influence of desire: good to eat, then capable of bestowing perspicacity, of conferring on the one who eats it certain attributes of the divine model. These attributes that God is keeping for Himself explain the prohibition: He wants to deprive human beings of them!

Here, the forbidding, the taboo, is sanctioned by a threat: death. But this is dismissed by the serpent, who relativizes the prohibition by putting God on the same level as humans: it is not to enable humans to avoid death, and therefore in their interest, that the rival declares that fruit off-limits to them; it is to keep a privilege for himself, the knowledge of good and evil that the fruit confers and that is a divine attribute, an attribute of the very being of the rival. Mimetic desire is born from the imitation of the model's desire. The objects that are most desired by the model, to which he holds on most tightly, are those he is keeping for himself, that he forbids. Mimetic desire becomes fixated, then, on the obstacle, on the prohibition, and the more the obstacle resists, the more frenzied the desire becomes.

In the interdividual relation between the self and the model, the vector running from the self to the model is a *vector of imitation*. The self imitates the model. This imitation bears first on his appearance, on the model's gestures and words. Then it comes to bear on the being itself of the model. The vector that runs from the model to the self is a *vector of suggestion*. Imitation and suggestion are correlative with one another.

In this case, the model, God, does not suggest anything at all; quite the contrary, he only counsels warns, points out the order of things. The God-man relation, unlike interhuman relations, does not involve potential reversals of the directions of the vectors. It is not a horizontal but a vertical relationship, in which the vectors remain always fixed as follows:

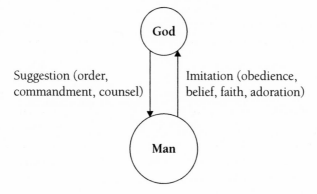

Figure 3

The vector running from God to man never reverses direction and becomes imitation. The vector running from man never turns into suggestion.

Moreover, an order differs from a suggestion: to carry out an order, one must remember that one is doing so. To carry out a suggestion, on the other hand, one must forget the suggestion during the process of imitation that follows from it: we appropriate to ourselves the action or thought that has been suggested to us, while forgetting that it comes from another. We believe that we have initiated it all by ourselves. Even when we act in the manner of an automaton under the influence of a model, we claim that we are autonomous.

Nevertheless, God cannot neglect to *put us on guard,* warning His creatures about the consequences of their actions, and it is by giving a twist to that warning that the serpent is able to substitute his own suggestion for the order given by the model. First he directs his suggestion to what the model has, then to its being, in order to elicit imitation. But that by itself would not be enough. What the serpent has to propose to Eve in order to stimulate desire in her, to get her moving psychologically, is the imitation of a desire. Because mimesis can bear on appearance, on having, on being, and finally on *desire.* At the terminal point of this mimetic sequence, the desire of the model's desire becomes a quasi-hypnotic form of imitation. Eve imitates less the desire of the serpent than yields as though in a blissful dream to the sudden desire she feels for divinity:

> So she took some of its fruit and ate it. She also gave some to her husband
> who was with her, and he ate it. (Gen. 3:6)

Eve has done the deed! Before going further and analyzing the consequences of her deed, let us reflect on the manner in which the serpent has been able to bring it about and on the mechanisms at work in it.

The relation between God and Eve:

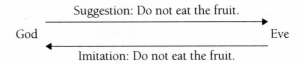

Figure 4

The interdividual relation between Eve and the serpent:

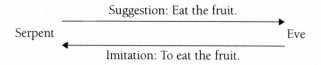

Figure 5

To render his own suggestion as powerful to her as that of God, the serpent puts himself, after a fashion, in the place of God: he already knows the difference between good and evil, and he knows what is going to happen to Eve if she eats the fruit. Thus he situates himself on God's level with regard to knowledge. His suggestion can then substitute itself for God's and essentially eclipse it.

But that would not by itself be sufficient if the serpent's lie did not manage to deform the shape of the problem. This lie consists in making her believe that God desires that particular tree because it confers on Him divine knowledge and power and that it is because He desires it that he wants to hold it back from Adam and Eve—rather than to protect them from death. From this point on, in desiring the tree, Eve imitates what she thinks is the desire of God; she appropriates God's desire to herself and *sees* in the following manner what her interdividual relation with God has become:

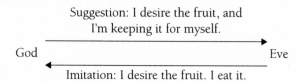

Figure 6

Her relation with God has become a simple interdividual relation. Transcendence has suddenly collapsed into immanence. What had been separation and contrast between the two suddenly turns into a mirage of fusion. The desire that has just been born, then, lacks the promise of eternity. Mimetic desire, represented here by the serpent, always operates in this way: when it begins to contemplate the object possessed by the other, it finds it "attractive, appetizing, interesting." Then, without noticing, it slips by way of imitation of the model's being into trying to appropriate his object. Sometimes, if the object is inaccessible, the imitator stops there, but more often he grabs the object, devours it, incorporates it, and then claims that he desired it before the model did.

By making Eve pass through the whole trajectory of mimetic desire, through a complete apprenticeship in the different forms of mimesis, and finally proposing to her that she become "like a god" by following his suggestion, the serpent guides her through all the stages of hominization.[23] That course of training culminates in, and is symbolized by, her eating the forbidden fruit and her bringing Adam to eat it also.

From a psychological point of view, the movement that has led Eve, and then Adam, to the act of transgression is purely mimetic. What is noteworthy is that it is not rooted in our biological makeup, nor in any instinct or need, nor in our essential identity.

Every Desire Is Rivalrous, and Every Rivalry Is Desirous

In the text we are studying, the mimetic movement is explicitly one of both desire and rivalry. Mimetic desire (the serpent) is not able to bring about the transition from possibility to the act except by creating the illusion that the Other (God) is the Rival who desires the object with such virulence that He forbids it to any other. The Biblical text can therefore be interpreted psychologically without that interpretation causing it to lose any of its power—quite the contrary.

- Desire is only mimetic. It is triggered only by imitation of the desire of the other, the model of desire.
- Desire appropriates for itself the model of desire before it appropriates the object.
- Mimetic desire can ultimately cause the transition to an actual deed only by inciting rivalry with the model; it must make me think that by keeping from me the object he forbids to me, the model keeps back for himself some additional degree of being, a knowledge and power that he deprives me of. He is therefore my rival and the cause of injury to me.

In sum, the Bible tells us, desire and rivalry are indissociable: mimetic desire creates rivalry, and rivalry exacerbates desire. Desire and rivalry are coextensive; these two dimensions are opposed, but indissociable. Both good and evil are contained in the same manner in the fruit that feeds, through their difference, the one who eats it. The difference between good and evil is at root that which constitutes and establishes desire: what is good is what I desire. What is bad is what my rival desires! Moral judgment follows along *afterward* to dress up the mimetic mechanism. It is this that makes that tree the tree of the knowledge of good and evil.

In the psychology of daily life, I desire the object that my model points out to me. The latter wants to keep it. He forbids it to me and thereby becomes my rival. In the text of Genesis, the object is forbidden before being desired. In forbidding that fruit, God wanted from the beginning to protect man from the mimetic poison, but He created him free, with all the consequences that can follow from that.

It is by making Eve believe that God has kept the object for Himself, and thus by inviting her to seek an increase of being, that the serpent draws forth her desire to model herself on the figure (actually invented by him) of God, to imitate the imaginary desire that is supposedly that of God Himself. Here God first becomes a rival, and only after that does He become a model. The lesson to be drawn from this is that rivalry can quite well precede desire and that one way or another, the two are inseparably linked. Rivalry is desire, and desire is rivalrous.

This tree, therefore, is truly the tree of the knowledge (in French, *connaissance,* which one could equally well write as *co-naissance,* i.e., "born together") of good and evil, which are separated only by a difference that is both mythic and venomous, the result of a mimetic process from beginning to end. The "forbidden fruit" is only a symbol, and it is mimetic rivalry, which is itself the source of all the oppositional differences in the world, that causes one to eat it. And yet these differences seem to come out of the "forbidden fruit" as though they were already contained in it before being swallowed by the humans who will never be able to digest them.

The allegory of the serpent is well chosen: the mimetic venom insinuates itself between the woman and God, then between the woman and the man. From this point on, false differences invade the field of reality, and reality is everywhere replaced by illusion. The world into which mimetic rivalry will plunge the man and woman is a world peopled with rivals who are equally models, and models who are equally rivals. Worldly desire transfigures the objects that the other's desire points it toward.

Allegorically speaking, the eating of the forbidden fruit has provoked the simultaneous birth (*co-naissance*) of good and evil. The difference constituted by these is illusory, and, contrary to what Eve thinks, to know it does not make her into the equal of God. God knows that that difference is fallacious, deceptive, venomous, and not created by Him. He sees what man has not seen since the beginning of the world: that the division between good and evil is the product of a diabolical enterprise, the result of the serpent's action, which subsequent tradition will rightly identify with the demonic, since the devil is an allegorical image of mimetic rivalry.

From now on, in the world Adam and Eve will find themselves plunged into, mimetic rivalry will produce violence, and the illusory distinction between good and evil will provide the justification of that violence: "my" desire will be presumptuously identified with the good, and the other's rival desire will mendaciously be identified with evil. In reality, however, these two desires are identical, since they are copied from one another! Only my failure to understand the truth of mimetic desire makes it possible for me to dress all of this in the costume of morality and to persuade myself that I alone incarnate the good.

Human beings will cling desperately to this lie, and the mechanism that blinds them is so powerful that there is every possibility that the reader, at this point in his or her reading, may already have forgotten that "my" desire and that of my rival are identical, are one and the same desire, because the one is copied from the other, both imitated and suggested by one another.

In the world that Adam and Eve enter, mimetic rivalry will set all human beings against each other. Coveting the same object, animated by the same desire, individuals, then ethnic groups, then whole peoples will be the prisoners of violence. The frantic claiming of priority and anteriority for one's own desire against that of one's rival will bring with it increasingly exacerbated violence. And the false difference that supposedly "came out" of the original fruit will justify all forms of violence: "my" violence, the expression of "my" desire, will be good; the violence of my rival, the expression of "his" desire, will be evil. Individuals and peoples will all do battle in the name of the good; they will all be trying to carry out the will of God (so they will think!), while their rival, the representative of evil, will be a minion of Satan, even as both sides are laying exclusive claim to what is, in reality, only one and the same desire!

Rival desires, because of their mimetic nature, are in fact identical. Rivalry and violence become exacerbated by their similarity and maintain themselves by means of self-misunderstanding.[24] That failure to understand is what reinforces their conviction: my desire is good, the other's desire is evil. And it is by grace of that misunderstanding and that illusion that violence dominates the world and gradually draws humanity into endlessly renewed conflicts.

Gandhi had a sense of that reality, and he tried to dissipate the misunderstanding and reveal the original illusion by designating violence itself as the evil and the enemy to strive against, rather than the English colonizers, who were only the receptacle of that evil. During his famous fasts he denounced and condemned violence on both sides in order to awaken Hindus and Muslims and appeal to them to stop their interethnic massacres, without trying to judge either of them. And because he sensed that all sexual relations involve a dose of rivalry and aggression that is susceptible of degenerating into violence, he also renounced having sexual relations with his wife: during their wedding ceremony, they therefore promised to love each other all their lives while withdrawing from any carnal possession of each other in order to completely liberate love from desire and no longer be dominated by it.

Girard has written splendidly about the passion of Christ as a revelation, recognition, and condemnation of violence as an absolute evil beyond any distinction between ordinary good and bad. Jesus was, as everyone can recognize, an innocent and arbitrary victim, designated as a victim by the madness of humans. The injustice of his death reveals the victimizing process and the fundamental innocence of the victim. It denounces and defuses the violence against him. It is always the failure to properly understand mimetic desire that leads human beings to the worst forms of violence. Hence the bitter statement of Christ in the moment of his death: "Father, they know not what they do!"

This statement is not a moral judgment, but a psychological diagnosis, and the diagnosis masterfully sums up the failure to understand, which is the result of mimetic rivalry, the consequence of the forbidden fruit.

The False Genesis of Good and Evil

The differences created by human beings and that mimetic rivalry has made emerge from the tree are now laid claim to by the human mind. From this point on they form a part of humanity itself. They begin by dividing God and man so that they are no longer able to dwell together in the same world: we behold the man and woman driven out of the paradise of immutable, perennial, stable differences into a world of subjective, rival, unstable, constantly changing differences that generate anguish, conflicts, and violence.

Henceforth human beings will remain perpetually deaf to the counsel of God that warned them not to swallow false differences, not to eat the fruit from that tree, which once eaten, creates a mendacious difference with "diabolical" effects: the difference of good and evil—something that has not been created by God, who has already created all that he judges necessary to humans—issuing from and caused by a process that is strictly mimetic and rivalrous. From that time on, this diabolical process has gone by the name of "the Prince of this world."

Ever since their origin, these unstable differences have had a further characteristic: they can be mixed together and confused. They ceaselessly blend into one another, often rendering the world opaque, incomprehensible, and therefore disturbing. This is why human beings rush to judgment, trying to distinguish true from false, to separate good from evil, to declare what is good and what is wicked. But the constant mixing of good and evil seeps into the judges themselves so that their judgment will often be unrighteous and unjust, seeking out a culprit or, quite often, even inventing one.

Christ, on the other hand, is much more radical: "Judge not, that you be not judged." In this saying, it is the very act of judging—judging with our relative and often self-interested criteria—that he condemns, not this or that particular judgment.

The strength of the judgment of Solomon came precisely from the fact that it did not proceed from an act of judging: the king's wisdom consisted of proposing that the mothers share the object of rivalry, which would itself have had the effect of killing the child to give each of them a half. By this judgment, Solomon put the two mothers in the position of having to choose between their mimetic rivalry and the life of the child. The bad mother chose triumph, chose to make her own rivalrous desire prevail over that of her rival, to the detriment of the child. She thus demonstrated strikingly that what really interested her was only winning a victory over her rival by depriving her rival of her son. On the other hand, the true mother showed who she was by being willing to let go of her rivalry, to give up any victory as long as that would keep the child safe. Let him belong to the rival, but let him live! By her choice of nonviolence and the preservation of life, she showed to the king and to all who were present that she was the true mother of the child. From then on, Solomon no longer had any "judgment" to bring. All he had to do was state the facts and let the rivals' attitudes speak for themselves. His wisdom consisted of creating the conditions necessary for the revelation of the mimetic rivalry, and of leaving to each of the women the responsibility for making her own choice.

Good and evil, in the psychological perspective we have adopted, are false differences that depend only on the point of view of the one who does the judging. These differences are the cause of the misery of the world, and they are at the root of all fanaticisms. Over the ages, they have "overlaid" the mechanism of mimetic desire to the point of hiding it completely, thereby replacing a misunderstood psychological reality with moral judgment, which will always appear "unjust" to the one who is condemned.

"And they realized that they were naked . . ."

The emergence of mimetic desire takes away from us our innocence, our peace, our happiness. Innocence stands in a very particular relation to mimetic rivalry: either innocence lies upstream from mimetic rivalry, or else it lies downstream from it, once innocence has been lost. Innocence is the absence of mimetic rivalry in a relationship. Thus small children, who have not yet entered into rivalry, preserve that innocence. If they want a piece of cake or a toy that their neighbor has, they don't proceed further; they don't yet develop strategies or conscious schemes for getting the object of their desire. They thus manifest little or no rivalry. A grown couple, on the other hand, once they've left behind their initial state of romantic fusion, will have to step carefully to avoid the snares that desire lays in their path, even if only to try to stay together. The birth of mimetic desire, after the excitement of their initial encounter, is the birth of a danger. This danger threatens *all* couples, just as it has from time immemorial threatened all human groupings not yet protected by rites and cultural institutions. The only way to protect the original spark of love is to understand the tricks and turns of the serpent, that "most naked" animal, who worms his way between the woman and God, between the man and the woman, and whose mimetic venom is allegorically represented by the forbidden fruit that humanity, ever since that time, has never been able to digest.

Adam and Eve, from that time on, are no longer *one,* but *two;* each withdraws into solitude.

> Then the eyes of both of them were opened and they realized that they were naked. So they sewed fig-leaves together to make themselves loin-cloths. (Gen. 3:7)

The couple has become disunited. The lovers *perceive* themselves as different. This is an optical illusion, but a psychological reality produced by mimetic desire. Moreover, as they are coming to learn, difference engenders rivalry, and the rivalrous difference they see coming into view between them terrifies them. And so, in a final, touching attempt to efface that difference, to hide it and return to the absence of difference that had been the couple's paradise, they make themselves loincloths in an effort to cover up the difference that from now on will separate them.

A moment ago they were naked, but they felt no shame before each other. Now that they are moved by desire, *all* their ways of relating to each other are impregnated with desire and rivalry and have become ambivalent. This is why Adam and Eve feel shame and *hide themselves.* Mimetic desire—manifesting itself in envy, jealousy, pride, and so on—is a sentiment that tries to cover itself up.

It is not only the sexual relation that one tries to hide from view. Adam and Eve hide from one another behind fig leaves, but they also try to hide themselves from God. The next verse says this explicitly, while telling us in passing that fear is born after the birth of desire and flows from it:

> The man and his wife heard the sound of Yahweh God walking in the garden
> in the cool of the day, and they *hid* from Yahweh God among the trees of the
> garden. (Gen. 3:8; my emphasis)

Nakedness represents the absence of protection, exposure to rivalrous
desire. The serpent was, let us not forget, "more naked than any living beast
of the field."

> But Yahweh God called to the man. "Where are you?" he asked. "I heard the
> sound of you in the garden," he replied. "I was afraid because I was naked,
> so I hid." (Gen. 3:9–10)

God immediately makes a diagnosis: this sense of nudity is not "natural,"
it is "cultural"; it comes from the other, it proceeds from otherness, *as does
desire*. The Bible is explicit about this:

> "*Who told you* that you were naked?" he asked. "Have you been eating from
> the tree I forbade you to eat?" (Gen. 3:11; my emphasis)[25]

Only mimetic desire could stimulate psychological movement in Adam
and make him disobey the source of his being and eat from the forbidden
tree. This is why God directs the full weight of his question toward the *mediator*: "Who?" He does not ask, "What happened in your head, in your heart?"
Still less does he ask, "What was going on in your unconscious?" Rather he
asks, "*Who* taught you?" If there is a mediator, the conclusion follows of itself:
"*Therefore* you have eaten of the tree of which I forbade you to eat!"

This is more a declaration than a reprimand. God's wrath is directed
toward the mediator, the obstacle, the *skandalon*,[26] (literally, the "stumbling-
block") that trips us up—the Tempter. God then proceeds to judge and punish
the mediator, but with regard to the man, God simply declares his entry into
the world of mimetic desire, with all the consequences that that will entail.

Adam's response is worth noting:

> The man replied, "It was the woman you put with me; she gave me some
> fruit from the tree, and I ate it." (Gen. 3:12)

To God's precise question of "Who?" Adam answers immediately with
a lie and an accusation: he accuses the woman of having "given him from
the tree,"[27] and he throws part of the responsibility back on God Himself for

having "put her with him." He is already living in the world of mimetism and prevarication, and so he unloads his guilt onto the first victim who falls to hand. In answer to God's question "Who taught you that you were naked?," Adam attributes the guilt to a person who did play a role in the proceeding, but who is not the "who" God was asking about.

Citing Rabbi Abba, Armand Abecassis translates Adam's answer as: "I ate and I will eat." In other words, Adam realizes that from now on he is in the grip of mimetic desire and that its action will begin again and again. Abecassis adds:

> Adam's story is not an accident that happened outside us; it will reproduce itself endlessly. Each of us is Adam, Eve, and the serpent. . . . The story of Paradise describes our nature and brings our weakness to light.[28]

Having "eaten" and swallowed difference, the lever that mimetism uses to set us in motion, Adam and Eve will be henceforth and forever its slaves: they have entered the world.

The text of Genesis subsequently reestablishes the idea of a role for transcendence in human desire. If mounting mimesis produces the sacred as a form of false transcendence ("you will be like gods"), only a true understanding of the mechanisms of desire will make it possible for the man and woman to grow in respect for each other. This false transcendence produces humanity, but it is an imperfect humanity that needs education and guidance in order to recover the innocence that it was its fate eventually to lose. As Paul Ricoeur says:

> In telling of the fall as an event, springing up from an unknown source, [the myth] furnishes anthropology with a key concept: the *contingency* of that radical evil which the penitent is always on the point of calling his evil nature. Thereby the myth proclaims the purely "historical" character of that radical evil; it prevents it from being regarded as primordial evil. Sin may be "older" than sins, but innocence is still "older."[29]

The myth bears witness therefore that "sin is not our original reality, does not constitute our first ontological status."[30]

"I shall put enmity between you and the woman . . ."

In response to God's questioning, the woman, too, accuses mimetic desire and the influence of a third party:

> Then Yahweh God said to the woman, "Why did you do that?" The woman
> replied, "The snake tempted me and I ate." (Gen. 3:13)

God then pronounces what might appear to be a sentence upon the three
actors, but it is really only a description of what awaits them in the adult
world, the mimetic world of desire that they are entering. The text ends with
a diagnosis, some predictions, and an expulsion.

The diagnosis:

> Then Yahweh God said, ". . . the man has become *like* one of us in knowing
> good from evil . . ." (Gen 3:22, my emphasis)

God diagnoses it as a case of incomplete hominization. The "like one of
us" refers less to the image of God than to His simulacrum. What man has
acceded to is only an illusory and deceptive difference; from here on, he will
be the prisoner of the rivalrous differences whose venom filled the forbidden
fruit. This is why I have underlined the "mimetic" diagnosis God gives: "The
man has become *like* one of us. . . ." He has not *become* one of us. He remains
only a copy, an imitator, and his discovery of good and evil only makes him *as
though* he were a god. This is a mimetic and even a diabolical illusion, of which
the man will from now on be the puppet and the prisoner, convinced that he
is himself good and on the side of the good and that the evil he is fighting
against is to be found only in the other. He will see very well the "mote" that
is in the eye of his neighbor, but not the "beam" that is in his own. He will
be expelled from Paradise and separated from God, Who Himself will not
be involved in the conflicts whose emptiness He sees, and Who "causes his
sun to rise on the bad as well as the good, and sends down rain to fall on the
upright and the wicked alike" (Matt. 5:45).

God, in creating, has established real, stable differences that are immutable and perennial. Man, moved by mimetic rivalry, creates artificial differences that are imaginary, unstable, ever in motion, and that all by themselves
generate rivalries, conflicts, and violence: the good and the bad, the beautiful
and the ugly, the normal and the abnormal, and so on.

Mimetic desire is therefore at the root of cultural, artificial, arbitrary
differences, and of rivalries. The production by mimetic rivalry of a relative
distinction between good and evil precedes all the differences that it subsequently creates. It is from the mimetic mechanism as such and from the need
to justify the preeminence of one's own desire over that of another that these
arbitrary notions and sources of violence are born.

God did not really forbid His creatures to eat from the tree, nor did He single out a forbidden fruit; rather, He only warned them, putting human beings on guard against mimetic temptation.

After having made His diagnosis, God drew the inevitable consequences from what has just happened. He predicts that from now on mimetic rivalry will constitute the essence of human relations—between the man and woman, of course, and also between human beings and nature.

The first and most important of God's predictions, with respect to the psychology that interests us here, is that which he addresses to the serpent:

> Then Yahweh God said to the snake, "Because you have done this, accursed be you of all animals wild and tame! On your belly you will go and on dust you will feed as long as you live. I shall put enmity between you and the woman, and between your offspring and hers; it will bruise your head and you will strike its heel." (Gen. 3:14–15)

If my hypothesis that the serpent is an allegory of mimetic desire is correct, this text can be read in that light. In the first part of this passage, God singles out the serpent from all other animals, domestic or wild. It is no longer an animal like any other, if it ever was that: it is cursed, separated out, pointed at, condemned to crawl on its belly and eat the dust of the earth, that is, to sneak around and slither silently among humans, insinuating itself between them, ready at any moment to attack them, striking at their heels. Certainly the heel is the logical place for a crawling creature to aim at to inject its venom. But it is also the least protected part of the body, the weak point of each of us, the place where mimetic desire can most easily penetrate and invade us.

Foreseeing that it will be at their weakest, least defensible point, their "Achilles heel," that the descendants of Eve will be most susceptible to temptation—that is, to the mimetic venom, to rivalrous passion, the desire to have what the other has and be what the other is—God describes in advance the human condition and the functioning of mimetic desire. This way of reading the text is supported by the Ten Commandments that were given to Moses, whose purpose was to counteract as much as possible the devastating effects of mimetic desire and rivalrous passion.

The text of Genesis indicates clearly that it is on his venom-bearing head that one must strike the serpent, the place where the mimetic poison is held ready for injection into one's heel, into mankind's point of greatest vulnerability—his deep sense of ontological lack, which makes him want to fill it with the "being" of the other.

After having declared in this way that mimetic desire will never let go of humanity again, God addresses the woman:

> To the woman he said: "I shall give you intense pain in childbearing, you will give birth to your children in pain. Your yearning will be for your husband, and he will dominate you." (Gen. 3:16)

[handwritten annotation: ➤ desire/own you, instead of love purely.]

Here God describes the ravages that will be produced by desire within the union of the couple. The mythic couple, united, paradisal, formed of two halves pervaded with mutual otherness, has disappeared. Desire and rivalry will henceforth be the dominant factor in their relationship. The woman will be impelled toward her husband by "yearning" (*convoitise*), that is, by desire that results from a mimetic and cultural movement, no longer by a natural appetite in the freshness of what had been the simultaneous creation of the two elements of the couple.[31] As for the man, he will dominate, "lord it over," his wife, with all the conflicts that such domination can give rise to.

The "covetousness," "domination," and rivalry now installed within the couple's relationship will govern all their ways of relating to one another from now on. Mimetic desire, the serpent, has now insinuated himself between the two lovers, and the venom of mimetic rivalry will forever poison their relationship.

"Accursed be the soil because of you!"

For the Bible, as for Plato, perfect love—love that is total, absolute, and fusional, in which the lovers form one person—is a mythic aspiration. Here, there, today, tomorrow, I will meet my other half, my *alter ego;* I will recognize in him or her the portion of otherness that is in me and the portion of myself that is in him or her. If that could really be possible, we would then—briefly!—be a couple alone in the world: we would be in paradise.

But Genesis teaches us that such fusional, pacific, happy, paradisal love is situated upstream from desire, in a time beyond time in which desire has not yet been born, and that this sort of illusion is condemned to be destroyed by the rivalry that will eat away little by little the relationship at the heart of the couple. Once serene love has become replaced by the "covetousness" of the one and the "domination" of the other, the Edenic relationship degenerates into a relationship of power.

There is a wealth of literature describing love that is mythic and ideal. There is even more of it describing the type of passion that is fed by rivalry, in which the loved one loses his or her status as a subject, one's other half, and becomes an object of desire, the stake of rivalrous competition, and ultimately the third pole of a "French triangle" (husband, wife, lover), as James Joyce so felicitously put it.

Finally, God addresses the man and for the first time gives a basis for his prediction: Adam, instead of following the commandment of God to take as a model Him alone, has taken as his model the woman, whom his mimetic choice is going to transform into a rival:

> To the man he said, "Because you listened to the voice of your wife and ate from the tree of which I had forbidden you to eat, Accursed be the soil *because of you!*" (Gen. 3:17, my emphasis)

Here, it is primarily mimetic desire itself that is condemned and held responsible for the curse that will fall on the earth: "You listened to the voice of your wife rather than to my voice, and you have therefore modeled your desire on hers; with this you have plunged into the downward spiral of mimetic desire, and it is from that that all your troubles will now flow." In addition to the rivalry and conflictual tension that will set the man and his wife in opposition to each other, there will also be a daily struggle with the earth for subsistence:

> Painfully will you get your food from it as long as you live. It will yield you brambles and thistles, as you eat the produce of the land. By the sweat of your face will you earn your food, until you return to the ground, as you were taken from it. For dust you are and to dust you shall return. (Gen. 3:17–19)

After these predictions addressed to each of the three actors in this drama, God pronounces the *expulsion*. But we must note that these predictions are not punishments; in reality, they are simply prophesies or attestations—expressions recognizing the reality that now is and will be henceforth. God is not *angry* with Adam and Eve. He keeps all His love and His solicitude for them. He pities them, one might say, and is deeply concerned about their fate. This is clear from the fact that

> Yahweh God made tunics of skins for the man and his wife and clothed them. (Gen. 3:21)

God clothes them and covers them before sending them off into the world, and if he dismisses them from the Garden of Eden, He will nevertheless continue to accompany them, as the Bible bears witness.

The Entry into Time

In the moment in which He casts them into the world, He inscribes in the man and woman, so as to complete their hominization, the temporal dimension of what I have called universal mimesis. Entering the world of difference, rivalry, and desire, Adam leaves the paradise of peace, harmony, and unity. He also leaves the eternity of the blessed instant and enters into time. God, a few lines further on, declares this:

> Then Yahweh God said, "Now that the man has become like one of us in knowing good from evil, let him not reach out his hand and pick from the tree of life too, and eat and live for ever!" (Gen. 3:22)[32]

For man to be deprived of the tree of life and of eternity is for him to enter into time, to find inscribed in himself the temporal dimension of mimesis. Indeed, time does not exist in human experience except in the form of memory. And memory is mimetic; it is the capacity to repeat, to reproduce what one has already experienced. This back-and-forth movement between the present and the past is an effort of restoration, an imitation of past images re-presented in consciousness. But as in spatial mimesis, the transfer of information from "earlier" to "later" brings with it modifications and deformations, losses of information and additions. *or cost/ late gain-*

Ever since man left paradise he has dreamed of returning there. Ideologies have proliferated that promise to provide his good and his happiness by eliminating those who, according to them, embody evil. But that ambition is in vain, since it is founded on a denial of reality: primal happiness, fusion, the perfect union of the couple, paradise—these all existed before man ate the fruit of the tree that held difference within it. Once difference was liberated by mimetic rivalry, it invaded the entire field of reality and brought to birth a new world. It brought with it the *co-naissance,* the knowledge and the co-birth, of good and evil. Ever since that has happened, we can no longer go back and expel that difference, empty our world of it, despite the violent and bloody efforts of various ideologies. All we can do is try to understand its illusoriness and its ever changing shapes. The most we can do now is try to accept reality

we have to try a lot harder.

and strive for wisdom. We must hope that humanity will eventually manage to digest that fruit and accept the fact that all evil is mixed with good, just as all good is mixed with evil. We must accept the reality that mimetic desire is the fuel of psychological movement, but we must at the same time reject the dishonest moral self-justification that would assimilate all our desires to "the good" while assimilating all those of the other to "evil." Simply to understand the concept itself of mimetic desire will be a first step on the path to enlightenment, since through it we can know that "my" desire and "his" are copied from one another, that in reality they are identical.

"If you hadn't talked with the snake, we'd be in Paradise now, eating the delicious fruit of the Garden of Eden, slaking our thirst with cool water, and we'd be happy," says Adam, sweating and pushing a plow.

"If you're so smart, why didn't you argue with Serpent yourself? Were you afraid? What a coward you are."

"Look at the state we're now in because of you and this Serpent of yours. We're hot, we're cold, we're sweaty and tired! Look at you: you're dirty, you're dressed in rags, your hair's a mess. I can't even recognize you any longer."

"You'd do better to keep pushing that plow instead of badmouthing me. Besides, you're the one God condemned to plow the earth, not me."

"And you—he said you'd bear children in pain. That's not going to happen any time soon, seeing as how you don't even want me to touch you any more."

"So what if I don't? I work myself to death all day long trying to keep house in this shack you like to say you 'built,' and in the evening, when you come back dirty, stinking, and worn out, I'm still supposed to make love with you?"

That very evening, when Adam returns to the hut, he has stopped on the way for a long bath in the river. He's combed his hair as best he could and carries a bouquet of flowers for Eve. She feels a sense of triumph and smiles. "Now I have him," she thinks to herself. She takes him by the hand and draws him to the bed: "OK, come on . . ."

Adam lies in the dark with his eyes open, thinking, "From now on, I'll have to seduce her each time. Once our embraces contained a taste of eternity. Whatever it might be, from now on I'm going to have to be careful what I say. I don't want trouble. Besides, we're alone now in a hostile world. Everything is against us: time, nature, the animals. I'm going to have to try to keep everything under control, even Eve as well . . . I don't know if I can handle it, I'm so tired."

Adam plunges into a deep, dreamless sleep. Eve is lying awake. She savors her triumph and rejoices in having set him straight. "But I have to be careful, even so; he's stronger than I am, and I need him for heavy labor and to get me food. But I'm not finished yet: I'm going to have children, children who will be mine, who will be allies for me, who will understand me and defend me."

Enchanted by this vision, and resolving to manage Adam and keep him under her spell, Eve falls asleep feeling pleased with herself.

"They know not what they do . . ."

From the psychological point of view, what must be emphasized about the moment when Adam and Eve leave Paradise behind is that they never really know why they've been expelled. They imagine that God has "punished" them for having disobeyed. They have no understanding at all of the mechanism that has been governing their psychological movements, that has destroyed their union, produced the difference between them, and set them apart from each other and from God. They think the serpent gave them some bad advice and that it is all his fault. In reality, rivalrous desire is now, and perpetually, working inside them to divide them in every moment and in every respect, and to separate and divide their numerous descendants, beginning with their sons, Cain and Abel.

The birth of desire and of human psychology goes hand in hand with ignorance and misunderstanding of the mimetic mechanisms that give birth to them. Blinded by these mechanisms, Adam and Eve left reality behind in order to enter into illusion, and their offspring still continue, in the world we now live in, to be the puppets of their illusions; in every moment and in every circumstance, "they know not what they do," as Christ cried out to his Father before dying on the cross (Luke 23:34).

Christ's prayer, asking forgiveness for those who crucified him, is remarkable in two ways. First, it contains no moral judgment; Christ does not say, "They are wicked, they are jealous, they are violent," and so on. What he says is simply a psychological observation: "they know not. . . ." Second, it validates the Girardian notion of *méconnaissance* (mis-knowing, interpreting falsely). In the works of Girard, this notion is fundamentally sociological and has to do with the victimizing mechanism: "We have said that the ability of the victimage mechanism to produce the sacred depends entirely on the extent to which the mechanism is misinterpreted."[33]

It is imperative to recognize the fundamental role of false understanding in psychology and psychopathology. Therefore, I am going to try in the next chapters to show how refusal to recognize and properly understand the otherness of desire produces pathology, and how, on the other hand, a correct recognition of that otherness can be therapeutic.

Universal Mimesis

1. Some Precursors

It took only a few steps for me to arrive at the theory of imitation.

—*Franz Anton Mesmer*

What is it that makes for the cohesion of the human race? What can explain the way human beings take such an interest in each other and try to live together? What is it that both draws them together and pushes them apart, unites them and sets them in opposition to one another? These are questions that philosophers, anthropologists, and psychologists have been intrigued by for centuries. Each discipline has been exploring along its own lines the mysterious, universal attraction that human beings exert on each other, and each has tried to find its own answers. Some of the intuitions of those who have explored these issues in the past have foreshadowed a number of aspects of the mimetic theory, and in the light of it they can now be seen to have a new pertinence and significance. These intuitions invite us to press our own reflections further and to define more explicitly a general principle: the principle of "universal mimesis"—the mimetic principle from which none can escape and that, like the principle of universal gravitation that governs physical movements, is able to illuminate decisively a number of human phenomena that appear contradictory: love and hate, alliance and conflict, attraction and repulsion.

The Insights of Franz Anton Mesmer

In 1913, in his book *The Nature of Sympathy,* the philosopher Max Scheler posed the question of human cohesion in the following way: "It is only in the course of many years' work . . . , that we have come to realize the full force and meaning of what can be briefly described as the question as to the grounds of the nature, existence and knowledge of the ties of connection between the spirits and the souls of men."[1] He then sets out to try to discover what is

> the metaphysic of men's knowledge of one another, of what they can have in common—the problem, that is, of how the deep-lying ontological and epistemological relations among men are adapted to the cosmic order, and of the types of human intercourse which that order permits and furthers, and those it does not. "This alone," Scheler says, "is what ultimately determines the nature and significance of man for his fellow men."[2]

A little before this, Scheler presented a remarkable intuition about the phenomena we are concerned with here:

> A decisive factor in cultivating a capacity for identification with the cosmos is that sense of immersion in the total stream of life, which is first aroused and established among men in respect of their mutual status as individual centres of life. For it seems to be more or less a rule (of which we have as yet no further understanding) that the actual realization of the capacity for cosmic identification cannot take place directly in relation to external Nature, but is mediated indirectly, in that sense of unity between man and man. . . .[3]

This question of the cohesion between human beings has often been considered a metaphysical one. Schopenhauer believed that the phenomenon of sympathy reveals an underlying unity of being that is the source and common basis of all the innumerable selves. From this point of view, sympathy would be what shatters the appearance that holds us prisoner, and in virtue of which each of us considers his or her *self* to be something real and independent. Therefore, according to Schopenhauer, it is the sense of pity that enables us to feel in a directly intuitive way the unity of the cosmic ground that he calls the "Will."[4]

Henri Bergson also took an interest in the same questions:

The more physics advances, the more it effaces the individuality of bodies . . . bodies and corpuscles tend to dissolve into a universal interaction.[5]

One of his statements even echoes our own intuitions:

Yet *a beneficent fluid* bathes us, whence we draw the very force to labor and to live. From this ocean of life, in which we are immersed, we are continually drawing something, and we feel that our being, or at least the intellect that guides it, has been formed therein by a kind of local *concentration*.[6]

Bergson, as Pierre Montebello has indicated, belongs among those philosophers who, like Félix Ravaisson, Gabriel Tarde, and Friedrich Nietzsche, are oriented toward "a conception of being as relational (being as effort, difference, will to power, duration)."[7] These philosophers believed it possible "to rediscover the creative flow of forces that pervades all things and to unite man with a power that courses through the world. What Ravaisson calls 'grace,' Bergson 'joy,' Nietzsche 'Dionysian yea-saying,' and Tarde 'harmonious hope,' constitute a form of ethic founded on the very meaning of the cosmos."[8]

Quite often, this sort of reflection on human cohesion extends to questions of the place of man in the universe and of the influence that the cosmos itself exerts on him. The "other metaphysic" reconstructed so convincingly by Montebello from the thought of these authors is a perfect illustration of such thinking:

This other metaphysic, neither rationalist, nor transcendental, nor relativist, seems the most human of all metaphysics of the cosmos, and the most cosmic of all metaphysics of man since the time of the Copernican revolution.[9]

A similar way of thinking about the universal interaction of human beings with each other or with the cosmos has been proposed and inquired into by many other thinkers and philosophers whom we could cite here. In psychology, on the other hand, the studies of Janet and later of Freud tended unfortunately to distance themselves from such thinking: both strove to locate within the *subject* some part of it, subconscious or unconscious, that governed its action. But it did not take long for Carl Gustav Jung to express once again that same fundamental intuition in his idea of a "collective unconscious," an immense reservoir from which the individual unconscious could draw; thus Jung revitalized and found a new formulation for the intuition that there is an underlying unity of human beings and universal communication between them.

* * *

Behind all of these thinkers who in their various ways anticipated the theory of psychological mimesis that I am here developing lay, as I explained in detail in my earlier book *The Puppet of Desire: The Psychology of Hysteria, Possession, and Hypnosis,* the eighteenth-century Viennese physician Franz Anton Mesmer.[10] Mesmer's hypothesis of a magnetic fluid that circulates throughout the universe and causes the hypnotic effects he summed up under the heading of "animal magnetism" was, whatever its scientific limitations, a bold and imaginative attempt to address serious questions about the inward forces that draw people together and lead them to engage in the sort of implicit imitation of the wishes of the hypnotist that he was observing.

He was also struck by the way the universality of the psychological effects of this force resembled those of the physical effects Sir Isaac Newton had not too long before described and explained in his theory of universal gravitation. In his *Dissertatio physico-medica de planetarum inflexu* of 1766, Mesmer wrote, "One must grant to Newton the greatest praise, because he has clarified to the highest degree the reciprocal attraction of all things," and went on to say, "Let us see to what extent this system can be accommodated to our own views and conformed to both reason and experience. . . ."[11]

The idea of a universally pervasive magnetic *fluid* that Mesmer developed he thought of as an amalgam of Newtonian motion, the physical properties of electricity and magnetism, and his own psychological observations of the attractions that human beings exert on one another. This blending, or even confusion, of physics and psychology bears witness simultaneously to the genius of Mesmer, who was early in bringing to light the analogies among these diverse phenomena, and to his limitations.

This, however, had the unfortunate effect that when Mesmer's detractors later proved the *physical* nonexistence of this magnetic fluid, that alone was sufficient to discredit Mesmer's entire theory among the thinkers of his time and delay for more than two centuries any further effort to develop a comprehensive and scientific physical explanation for the psychological phenonemena he had astutely identified and had at least made an initial attempt to find an explanation for. Mesmer saw correctly, however, that the fundamental problem in psychology is that of explaining psychological movement. He also saw correctly that this movement is communicated from one human being to another. As we shall see shortly, the recent discovery of mirror neurons now fulfills in a similarly comprehensive, but empirically as well as theoretically based way, that the universal force Mesmer had intuitively discerned is a reality, even if a reality of a neurological rather than planetary sort.

What I have said about this force so far has focused on the individual and on the dyad made up of imitator and model. The principle of universal mimesis pertains equally to the psychology of large groups, in a manner that the Newtonian analogy can help again to make clear.

Collective Psychology

Just as the force of attraction between two physical objects, in Newtonian gravitation, is directly proportional to their mass and inversely proportional to the distance that separates them from one another, so also is the force of attraction between two psychological subjects. If our hypothesis about the force of mimesis is correct, we should expect to find cases in human experience where the interaction of these two parameters, of mass and distance, brings about a dizzying increase in the attraction between subjects and consequently modifies radically the interdividual relation, to the point of nullifying all the laws of individual psychology.

Such conditions can be seen in the case of large gatherings of people, as Gustave Le Bon brought to attention in the nineteenth century when he developed the idea of a "psychology of crowds" and asserted that the phenomena of such group psychology were governed by completely different laws. Freud, too, devoted his *Group Psychology and the Analysis of the Ego* to this topic, where he recognized the pioneering work of Le Bon. More recently, Elias Canetti, in *Crowds and Power,* makes some similar observations.

For the present purpose, we must consider cases of such group phenomena in the light of the principles that I have proposed and see the extent to which these can prove explanatory.

In a crowd, the force of mimetic attraction is greatly magnified by the two parameters of mass and distance that determine it. On the one side, there is the increase of "mass," which in the case of large numbers of people is closely associated with quantity. This is one reason the psychology of the individual is different from that of groups, and all the more from that of crowds. In addition, there is also the dizzying reduction of the distance that separates the members of a crowd from one another. The very notion of a crowd is based on the extreme closeness of its members, which hurls them together and makes them lose their individuality as they begin to coalesce.

For these phenomena to manifest themselves, the individual subjects have to be "caught up" in the crowd. What is needed, as Le Bon would say, is that a heterogeneous, amorphous crowd be transformed into one that is homogeneous and active. For this movement from the habitual psychology of the individual to that of a crowd to take place, there must be the sort of mimetic triggering that Elias Canetti describes:

> The crowd, suddenly there where there was nothing before, is a mysterious and universal phenomenon. A few people may have been standing together—five, ten or twelve, not more; nothing has been announced, nothing is expected. Suddenly everywhere is black with people and more come streaming from all sides as though streets had only one direction. . . . It seems as though the movement of some of them transmits itself to the others. But that is not all; they have a goal which is there before they can find words for it.[12]

What is striking about this description by Canetti of the spontaneous generation of a crowd is the strictly mimetic manner in which it is constituted. The movements of some get communicated to others, and all rush toward the place of maximum mimetic density where the greatest number are becoming knotted together.

What Le Bon studied was the way crowds gather around ideas and beliefs and around the leaders who incarnate them. We can now see clearly, as René Girard has shown, that beliefs are basically forms of mimetic contagion, and that the leader who is able to assemble and incite a crowd is as much the crowd's product as he is its head.

Once the parameters of quantity and distance begin to move to extremes, the attraction exerted by the mass of the crowd increases exponentially. This is what Canetti observed, without yet being able to explain it:

> As soon as it exists at all, it wants to consist of more people: the urge to grow is the first and supreme attribute of the crowd. It wants to seize everyone within reach; . . . The natural crowd is the open crowd; there are no limits whatever to its growth.[13]

Canetti correctly observed the effects that a prodigious increase in mimetic attraction can have on any subject who passes near its mass, just as any body in space that passes by a more massive body can be drawn into its orbit.

But when they are inside the crowd, the subjects who undergo the effects of this kind of greatly intensified mimesis lose the individuality that made them psychological entities. They no longer obey the laws of individual psychology but those of group psychology. As Gustave Le Bon analyzed it:

> The most striking peculiarity presented by a psychological crowd is the fol-
> lowing: Whoever be the individuals that compose it, however like or unlike
> be their mode of life, their occupations, their character, or their intelligence,
> the fact that they have been transformed into a crowd puts them in posses-
> sion of a sort of collective mind which makes them feel, think, and act in a
> manner quite different from that in which each individual of them would
> think, feel, and act were he in a state of isolation. There are certain ideas and
> feelings which do not come into being, or do not transform themselves into
> acts except in the case of individuals forming a crowd. The psychological
> crowd is a provisional being formed of heterogeneous elements, which for
> a moment are combined, exactly as the cells which constitute a living body
> form by their reunion a new being which displays characteristics very dif-
> ferent from those possessed by each of the cells singly.[14]

Thus for Le Bon there was a psychological law of the mental unity of crowds.
I see that mental unity myself as the expression of mimetic contagion and a
dizzying increase in mimetic attraction.

In a crowd, the mimetic pull is such that abominable things become possible, things of which an individual alone would usually be incapable. Thus
it happens that "we are surprised / At the ease and speed of our deed / And
uneasy," like those W. H. Auden portrayed in his poem "Nones," who in the
morning had cried out for Jesus's crucifixion and then watched him die at
noon, but who at three in the afternoon scarcely remember who and what
they were in those events, so that:

> All if challenged would reply
> —"It was a monster with one red eye,
> A crowd that saw him die, not I"[15]

Here, individuality dissolves into mimetic interdividuality. There is no
longer an "I," but a "we," a diffuse cellular protoplasm whose nucleus has
lost all autonomy. The psychology in such a case becomes reduced to a
primitive state of coalescence, a stage preceding language. Language, I must
emphasize, serves to separate individuals more than to unite them and can
only enable them to communicate to the extent that it first separates them
from one another and confers on them a certain degree of autonomy and
existence.

Individuals in a crowd can take each other as models and let themselves
be drawn into the most insane actions. They can take any model at all as their

"chief" and follow him into any absurdity. They can also take each other as obstacles and rivals. Undifferentiated violence will then be unleashed in the crowd and usher in the sort of sacrificial crisis whose unfolding and resolution has been so masterfully described by Girard.

What the Book of Genesis showed us was that psychological movement is purely mimetic. Everything was fine in Paradise, but on the level of psychological movement nothing could happen without the intervention of desire. It was psychological movement, that is, desire, that ushered human beings into the world and into time. Time presents or expresses itself as movement. Without time, movement would be meaningless; without movement, time would not exist for anyone, because it would be imperceptible.

Time subsists by way of a perpetual double movement: universal gravitation in the physical world and universal mimesis in the psychological world. These two motions are rendered perpetual by the fact that they govern in accord with a single principle the interaction of physical bodies on the one hand and psychological entities on the other: the movement of bodies toward one another is deflected by the movement that separates them from one another. Thus physical and psychic bodies can neither simply wander off from one another nor collide and crush each other; they circle about each other perpetually. If a meteorite or other spatial object leaves the orbit that holds it, it is because it has been drawn into the orbit of another object with superior attractive force. If one subject becomes detached from another subject, it is because he or she has succumbed to the attraction of still another subject.

2. The Discovery of Mirror Neurons

The minds of men are mirrors to one another.

—David Hume

At this point in our reflections, we have defined desire as the force of movement in psychology. We adhere, with René Girard, to the hypothesis that desire is mimetic, and we have analyzed the interdividual relation, or mimetic rapport, as consisting of two vectors that move constantly back and forth: a vector of imitation and a vector of suggestion.

Girard formulated his hypothesis of mimetic desire in 1961. In 1971 I adopted that hypothesis myself and have worked with Girard since that time.

We published together the results of our anthropological and psychological research in 1978.[16]

But it was only at the beginning of the 1990s that our mimetic hypotheses were scientifically established as certain, thanks to the work of researchers at the Institute of Neurosciences at the University of Parma: Giacomo Rizzolati, Leonardo Fogassi, Vittorio Gallese, and their collaborators. It is they who discovered mirror neurons and thus validated the intuitions of all the thinkers and philosophers cited in the preceding section who had presentiments of, but not yet proof for, a mechanism of universal cohesion that could explain human interactions, sympathy, empathy, learning, communication, and language. As summed up by these Italian scholars, the principle is simple: "Certain brain cells called mirror neurons reflect the exterior world: they become activated when one performs an action and when one sees someone else perform one."[17] Vittorio Gallese describes this in further detail:

> About ten years ago we discovered in the macaque monkey brain a class of premotor neurons that discharge not only when the monkey executes goal-related hand actions like grasping objects, but also when observing other individuals (monkeys or humans) executing similar actions. We called them "mirror neurons." . . . The observation of an object-related hand action leads to the activation of the same neural network active during its actual execution. Action observation causes in the observer the automatic activation of the same neural mechanism triggered by action execution.[18]

The type of imitation that bears on appearance, this disposition to imitate the action one observes in another, is therefore neither facultative, something one does or does not do by choice, nor is it aleatory, something that depends on uncertain contingencies: it is neurological, automatic, and necessary. Professor Gallese, with whom I had a long discussion at Stanford in April 2007, recognizes that the Girardian idea of mimesis is confirmed by this discovery, although he himself uses the term *embodied simulation* to characterize the underlying process, rather than the Girardian terms *imitation* or *mimesis*.

Andrew Meltzoff, from the University of Washington in Seattle, who was also present at the same colloquium at Stanford, was enthusiastic about the way the discovery of mirror neurons confirmed the experiments made by his team since 1977 on newborn babies, some of whom were only a few hours old. These newborns imitated automatically such gestures of the experimenter as sticking out his tongue, for example, without the gesture having any particular meaning for them or being associated with any prior experience. Meltzoff received permission from one mother to perform the experiment with her baby when it was only a half hour old. Meltzoff's face was the first human face the infant had ever seen, even before that of his mother, and the result was conclusive: when Meltzoff stuck out his tongue, the newborn stuck his tongue out at him too.

The result of this experiment can only be understood if one knows that there exist, in the frontal motor areas of the brain, mirror neurons that become activated by the sight of an action performed by another human being and that light up, as seen with a PET-scan (positron emission topography), in the person who witnesses an action in exactly the same manner as they do in the person who performs it. These neurons in the motor and premotor areas remain silent in the presence of a movement done by a nonhuman or nonanimal: an automatic lever arm, for example, grasping some food will not stimulate the activation of mirror neurons in a monkey.

These observations establish indubitably that between humans there is:

- a cohesion, a tacit accord, neurologically inscribed in the brain, that transmits movement from one to the other;
- an awakening of mirroring motor areas in an observer that enables him to understand instantly, by automatic, necessary, neuronal transmission and communication, the meaning and intention of an action he observes.

Thus the premotor area F5 discharges strongly when a monkey sees a man's hand reach to grasp an object, although it does not discharge if the hand moves "gratuitously" without an object to grasp. Better yet: that same area F5 fires and discharges when the monkey sees the hand of the experimenter disappear behind an opaque screen if the monkey has previously seen some item of food, such as an apple, put in that place before the experimenter hid the object behind the screen.

Gallese's conclusion is that it is not only the movement that is communicated from the man to the monkey, but also the *intention*. That intention, communicated from one to the other as it is picked up by the mirror neurons of the observer, triggers a discharge of mirror neurons in the same zone of the brain in the observer as in the brain of the one who performs the act or displays an intention to perform it.

This confirms what Meltzoff found in some psychological experiments he describes as follows:

One study involved showing 18-month-old infants an unsuccessful act, a failed effort (Meltzoff 1995). For example, the adult 'accidentally' under- or overshot his target, or he tried to perform a behaviour, but his hand slipped several times; thus the goal state was not achieved. To an adult, it was easy to read the actor's intentions although he did not fulfil them. The experimental question was whether infants also read through the literal body movements to the underlying goal of the act. The measure of how they interpreted the event was what they chose to re-enact. In this case the correct answer was not to copy the literal movement that was actually seen, but to copy the actor's goal, which remained unfulfilled. The study compared infants' tendency to perform the target act in several situations: (i) after they saw the full target act demonstrated, (ii) after they saw the unsuccessful attempt to perform the act, and (iii) after it was neither shown nor attempted. The results showed that 18-month-old infants can infer the unseen goals implied by unsuccessful attempts. Infants who saw the unsuccessful attempt and infants who saw the full target act both produced target acts at a significantly higher rate than controls.[19]

In one experiment, a researcher showed eighteen-month-olds how he was trying to take one end off of a toy "mini-dumbbell." Instead of actually doing it, he pretended he couldn't succeed in getting it off. The children therefore never saw an exact *representation* of the goal of the action. Using different control groups, the investigators observed that the children had grasped the intention of the researcher (to remove the end of the dumbbell) and that they imitated that intention and not what they actually saw. Children therefore imitate not a representation but a goal, a purpose. As Meltzoff sums up his conclusion about these experiments: "Evidently, young toddlers can understand our goals even if we fail to fulfil them. They choose to imitate what we meant to do, rather than what we mistakenly did do."[20]

Children therefore can understand the intentions of adults even if those adults do not succeed in accomplishing those intentions. They imitate what the researchers *want* to do rather than what they actually *do*.

A second experiment was designed to find out if infants attribute motives to inanimate objects. For this test, the investigators constructed a small machine (with poles for arms and mechanical pincers for hands) that performed exactly the same abortive action as in the first experiment. It was quickly determined that infants who saw that demonstration were no more disposed to attribute an intention to the movements of the inanimate device when its pincers slipped off the ends of the dumbbell than were others who did not see the demonstration; they were no more (or less) likely to pull the toy apart after seeing the failed attempt of the inanimate device than they were when they saw nothing. It seems clear, therefore, that infants do not attribute intentions to inanimate objects.

A third experiment was designed to show to what extent children attend to the motives of those around them and how important such motives and intentions are to them. In this test, the ends of the little dumbbell were glued solidly to the bar so that they could not be removed. The researcher performed again the same demonstration as in the preceding experiments: he tried to remove the ends of the toy, but his hand slipped off. When the children tried, the same thing happened (since the ends were glued on), but they were not at all satisfied simply to reproduce what they saw the adult do. They tried again and again to take the end off, biting it and throwing beseeching looks at their mothers and at the researcher.

The work of Meltzoff reinforces the idea that children begin by focusing their attention on the goals of adults and not simply on their actions. Several scholars go still further and suggest that human imitation is always—on the most basic level—an imitation of intentions and goals rather than of actions and representations. This hypothesis (which is deduced from numerous empirical data that point toward that conclusion) has been dubbed the "goal-directed theory of imitation."[21]

What could indicate better than this that mimesis does not bear only on appearance, on gesture, or on having, but bears mainly and essentially, from the very earliest age, on intention, which is to say, on desire?

Mimesis that bears on having, the mimesis of appropriation, draws this comment from Giacomo Rizzolatti, the discoverer of mirror neurons: "The process of imitation is limited among monkeys, and it is often very dangerous for them to imitate."[22]

Why is imitation so dangerous? Let us remember that the neurons in the premotor cortex of the monkeys studied by Rizzolatti were activated when the animal made a movement with a precise goal, most frequently to pick up some object. Let us imagine now a monkey who tries to take possession of an object and another who imitates him blindly, automatically. The hands of those two animals converging on a single object cannot fail to provoke a conflict.

The neuronal "mirror" mechanism reveals not only the mimesis that bears on a gesture or on appearance, but also the mimetic desire itself, the mimesis that bears on the intention revealed by the gesture, on the desire that the gesture of appropriation exposes to view. The proof of this is that when the monkey knows there is nothing behind the screen, because he saw the screen being put in place, his premotor area remains silent as the hand of the experimenter reaches behind the screen.

Following the initial discoveries in Parma, research into mirror neurons is being very actively pursued in laboratories of neuroscience around the world. Mirror neurons are being discovered in numerous other zones of the human brain. Rizzolatti and Gallese particularly emphasize that the mirror neuron system includes Broca's area, the essential center of language, and they conclude:

> If, as some linguists think, human communication began with facial and hand gestures, then mirror neurons could have played an important role in the genesis and evolution of language. The mechanism of mirror neurons solves two fundamental problems of communication: equivalence and direct comprehension. Equivalence supposes that the meaning of a message is the same for both the sender and the receiver. Direct comprehension implies that it is not necessary that there be a pre-existing accord between the speaker and hearer for them to be able to understand each other: *the accord is inherent in the neuronal organization of the two parties.*[23]

And indeed there was no "accord" between Meltzoff and the half-hour-old infant. The neuronal organization of a neonate models itself quite naturally on that of the experimenter, "plugs into" it, and *imitates* his gesture.

Mirror neurons therefore demonstrate incontestably, on the PET-scan screen, that the mimesis bearing on appearance, gesture, and intention, and therefore on desire, is a neuronal mechanism inscribed in the brains of animate beings, and especially the human brain, and that this mechanism functions necessarily and automatically, so that psychological movement communicates itself from one subject to another without the least resistance. Mirror neurons provide an answer to the questions of all the thinkers who have wondered about the mysterious cohesion of human beings, including Mesmer, who clearly saw that movement passing from one to another and thought of it as "magnetic." Mirror neurons provide experimental demonstration of the central place mimesis occupies at the heart of psychology, and they prove that desire is mimetic, just as Girard postulated in 1961.

Perhaps mirror neurons will make it possible for our culture to accept the reality of mimetic desire and therefore the otherness of desire, because they will remove the issue of responsibility and guilt from desire, whose origin will no longer be hidden away in a part of the psyche arbitrarily isolated under the name of "the unconscious," but will finally be scientifically understood as located in the *other,* on the level of neurons and physiology. The PET-scan enables us, moreover, actually to see desire transmitting itself mimetically, as in a mirror, from one subject to another.

An additional experiment further confirms our claim: mirror neurons fire in the brain of a monkey who sees a man or another monkey take hold of a peanut and crack open its shell before eating its contents. The premotor area involved becomes activated even when the monkey only hears the cracking sound without seeing either the gesture or the experimenter. Now we are able to understand how, in the elaborately evolved brain of a human, a gesture, a sound, a glance, or an attitude can betray a desire that is immediately noticed by an observer. This contagious, mimetic desire no longer seems a mysterious "fluid," but is now known to be a neurophysiological reality.

The questions raised by Max Scheler concerning sympathy and empathy that were referred to in the preceding section also find their answers here. Vittorio Gallese writes:

> Our brains, and those of other primates, appear to have developed a basic functional mechanism, embodied simulation, which gives us an experiential insight of other minds. The shareability of the phenomenal content of the intentional relations of others, by means of the shared neural underpinnings, produces intentional attunement. Intentional attunement, in turn, by collapsing the others' intentions into the observer's ones, produces the peculiar quality of familiarity we entertain with other individuals. This is what "being empathic" is about. By means of a shared neural state realized in two different bodies that nevertheless obey to the same morpho-functional rules, the "objectual other" becomes "another self."[24]

Using slightly different terminology, Gallese echoes what I wrote myself in 1982 in *The Puppet of Desire.* I stressed at that time that our entry into human being, the interest in adults felt by children, and interhuman verbal and affective communication are universal, though with some exceptions, such as in the case of autism in particular, and both this universality and the exceptions to it are now able to be explained by the activity or failure of mirror neurons. Recent research demonstrates that autistics show reduced activity of mirror neurons in the frontal gyrus, a part of the premotor cortex, and this perhaps explains their inability to assess the intentions of others. In addition, a dysfunction of mirror neurons in the insular and cingular anterior cortex seems to be responsible for certain other symptoms such as lack of empathy.[25] Research on this is continuing, but we already know enough to completely remove guilt from the parents and especially the mothers of autistic children; it is not autistic children who must be pitied for having a "deficient mother," but the parents who are to be pitied for having a neurologically handicapped *disabled* child.

At the other end of life, in certain forms of frontal dementia, François Lhermitte has drawn attention since 1981 to the fact that cognitive loss can set loose in those suffering from dementia a purely imitative, mimetic activity of which they no longer understand the significance. In clinical neurological terms, these mechanical behaviors consisting of repeating the words or gestures of the examiner are called echolalia and echopraxy. When Narcissus is no longer there to drown in his own image, it is the nymph Echo alone whose voice reverberates in the void.

Something Professor Gallese said at the meeting at Stanford that has not yet been published is that the mirror system reacts and responds in an even livelier way when an element of competition accompanies the gesture or perceived intention. The mirror neurons of two monkeys fire in a particularly intense manner if they have to vie in speed with each other in order to seize the mouthful that is offered to them. Hearing Gallese speak of this, René Girard and I felt enthusiastic: he was telling us that it was now neurologically proven that rivalry intensifies and aggravates desire. Gallese accepted that way of stating what he meant and assured us that research into that issue is being actively pursued.

To sum up, the discovery of mirror neurons brings scientific proof that our system of mirror neurons, integrated into numerous—and perhaps all— parts of our brain, grasps the intention or desire of another whom we observe and begins to imitate it, modeling that desire in the same areas of our brain that, in the other, gave birth to it.

3. A NEW THEORY OF DESIRE

It is an undeniable and systematic fact that each time a self is forged in the interdividual relation by copying the desires of another, it immediately forgets the origin of its movements and the influence it is subject to and seeks to appropriate this origin to itself by claiming the anteriority of its desires over those of its model—and it does this with the confident feeling that it is acting in good faith. The self takes shape in misunderstanding of the very force that constitutes it and animates it. This misunderstanding is not only a source of illusions and endless errors about itself, but it also leads the self inevitably to make a rival of its model, an obstacle to which it will increasingly oppose itself in order to affirm its supposedly prior autonomy and better hide the truth of the mimetic relation, which would undermine its dream of power. This failure of understanding leads, then, to envy, to resentment, to hatred, and also to all sorts of pathology, as I will show in this section.

The other great illusion induced by the denial of mimetic desire—and the exposure of this illusion is one of the greatest lessons of the Bible—has to do with the object that the model designates for us. Mimetic desire, which is also rivalrous desire, progressively transfigures the object, and it does so all the more in proportion as we forget that it is only the prestige of the model that gives the object its aura. The tree in the Garden of Eden was distinguished from the others by the Model who forbade it, but it did not become "appetizing" and "desirable" until mimetic rivalry became fixed upon it. Then it took on a decisive importance and became the only object worthy of interest, worthy of being desired, to the degree that it seemed as if taking its fruit and eating it would guarantee an increase in being, the gaining of an ontological possession that the Model seemed to want to keep for Himself.

The object retains a place in interdividual psychology, but it can have only as much importance as mimetic rivalry gives to it; what attractiveness it possesses is conferred on it by the model insofar as, once it has been singled out by mimetism, it alone becomes what will satisfy one's desire. Substitute objects, equivalent and "permitted" though they might be, can satisfy only instincts and needs, not desire.

Desire, then, transfigures the object and both fools us and makes fools of us. The world in which we live is a world of illusion. To gain wisdom and peace, to escape from the rivalry that lies in wait for us, we have to see reality as it really is, to learn the truth about the mimetic desire that runs through us. Doing this is what, in *Evolution and Conversion*, René Girard calls "conversion."[26]

Interdividual psychology must be connected, therefore, with the study of all the types of illusion and all the distortions of reality generated by desire and by our misunderstanding of the nature of desire. What needs to be developed is a "metapsychology" of desire, in the sense in which Freud used that term to designate a more theoretical form of psychology, the establishing of conceptual models that can enable us better to understand the proper dynamics of desire and to deconstruct little by little the "metaphysical" illusions that accrue to it (such ideas as one's ownership of one's desire and of its autonomy, anteriority, and authenticity).

A Scientific Psychology

From the time of Plato until that of such nineteenth-century sociologists as Gabriel Tarde, imitation was viewed on the psychological level as simple copying, and on the sociological level as the production of conformism and uniformity. Imitation was seen as peaceful and nonviolent. Nobody before Girard emphasized the key role of imitation in the genesis of rivalries and conflict.

Suggestion was much discussed and written about, especially in France, where it was studied in isolation, from the time of Mesmer and Abbé Faria until Charcot, Janet, Bernheim, and Freud. That debate had to do with the relation between suggestion and hypnosis.

In reality, as I already said above, one must view the two phenomena of imitation and suggestion as the back-and-forth movement of the interdividual relation between subjects A and B:

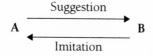

Figure 7

These two vectors constitute the interdividual relation A-B: they are of equal intensity, but moving in opposite directions. They are able to *reverse direction* over and over with enormous rapidity within the permanent framework of the relation between A and B. I must insist on this point: one may say of A that A has suggested a gesture to B only *to the extent that* B has imitated that gesture. Likewise, one may say of B that he has imitated a gesture of A only *to the extent that* A has effectively suggested that gesture. Imitation and suggestion are one and the same reality; the two vectors are indissociable. Every imitation becomes in its turn a suggestion that will be imitated, and so on. In the exchange between A and B, in the interdividual relation, the vectors of suggestion and imitation never cease to reverse themselves, and they often become indistinguishable, so rapid are their oscillations.

I have tried to show that, in the special form of the interdividual relation known as hypnosis, the vectors of imitation and suggestion can become fixed in a single direction (the major portion of suggestion in one direction and the major portion of imitation in the other) with the result that in the hypnotized person there is a great increase in suggestibility, that is, sensitivity to the

suggestion of the hypnotist, and also at the same time and in the same proportion, an increase in "imitativity," that is, the capacity to model oneself on the
desire of the hypnotist as that is revealed through his words or gestures.[27]

If one accepts the hypothesis of mimetic desire, it becomes clear that we
must abandon the idea that the self is the source of desire. Rather, it is the
movement of desire that gradually engenders in a subject a dynamic structure
that is both changing and persisting and that can be designated as the "self."
To understand this, we must develop new theoretical models of desire.

The self is not simply a prime datum drawing from its biological ground
the energy necessary for producing and maintaining a desire that only needs
to invest itself in something, to choose a goal for itself. On the contrary, it
is desire that gradually brings the self into existence by constituting it as a
self-of-desire.

The desire that constitutes the self is itself modeled on, copied from,
inspired by, and communicated by the other. It is the other's desire that causes
the desire to appear that will engender the self.

In physical time, the time of objective reality, of clocks and universal
gravitation, the sequence of events shows itself in the following manner:

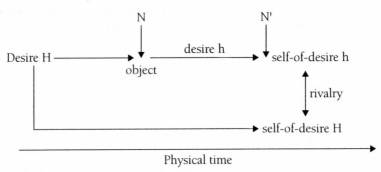

Figure 8

Here we see two subjects: "h" and his or her model "H," both of whom
desire the same object. There are two nodal points, N and N', representing
the self in the process of desire that generates it; these two successive states
are fundamental, because they are universal and common to all subjects. The
constancy of their presence is a basis for the hope for a scientific psychology
in which it will be possible to determine two constants:

- At point N: *desire* h claims to be prior to, earlier than Desire H, of which
  it is in reality a copy. At that same point, desire h discovers, to its great

surprise, that another desire than it, Desire H, has already fastened onto the object or project that desire h covets. Desire h, then, denying any evidence to the contrary, asserts forcefully, even violently, its claim to priority in relation to Desire H. It does so in good faith. But in doing this, it reverses the actual direction of time.

- At point N': *self* h claims ownership of "his" desire h, which has just constituted him. In all good faith, he, self h, vehemently asserts that his desire is his own, that he has produced it himself, that he is its owner, and that, at point N, he was quite surprised to see a rival desire H bearing on that object or that project that he had himself aimed at well before subject H had.

Interdividual psychology must therefore be the study of the strategies—normal, neurotic, or psychotic—set in motion by the *desire* at point N to claim its anteriority in relation to the desire it models itself on, and set in motion in turn by the *self* at point N', to claim the priority of "his" desire and therefore his own existential anteriority in relation to the desire of his model. The functioning of these two strategies results in turning around the physical order of things, which reverses the real sequence of events and therefore the direction of physical time, thereby creating a new time: *psychological time.*

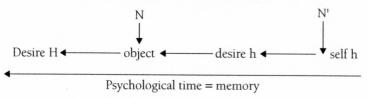

Figure 9

When psychological time is shown reversed in direction (as in this figure), one can see clearly that on the vector of psychological time the *self* h precedes the *desire* h, of which it claims ownership at point N', and one also sees that desire h bears upon the object at point N where it claims its own anteriority, its prior presence as compared with that of Desire H.

A New Anthropology

Memory is the guardian of the temple, because it makes possible forgetfulness! It allows self h to forget its origin and its formation, to forget how it was produced by desire h. It allows desire h to forget that it was produced by Desire H, of which it is only a copy. It is this double forgetting that makes possible the subsistence of the self.

Throughout this process, this sequence of events, the self and the desire are in full agreement; they share a common "interest" in reversing the real direction of the arrows. In reality, it could not be otherwise, for that reversal is what guarantees their very existence. That reversal of the order of time is the *third constant* of interdividual psychology (in addition to the constancy of the nodal points N and N'); that reversal is the condition that makes possible the ontological constitution of psychological subjectivity. This third constant is *memory,* which is in reality an elaborate machine for reversing the direction of time. The experience of each of us until now has been pointing to this fact, and the metapsychology that I am trying to put in place shows us its necessary character.

I would like here to explain briefly why hypnosis is the essential model of all psychotherapy: because the hypnotic rapport between H and h reverses the direction of the arrows once again and thereby reestablishes the true order of time. Hypnosis imposes at point N the reality of the anteriority of H's desire over that of h. This is only at a given moment, to be sure, but the demonstration of the real relation in that moment also serves as a revelation of all the past inversions of the true order. The person hypnotized actually experiences *in that moment,* in that particular context, the fact that his desire is really that of the hypnotist, even if he will more or less forget that experienced reality on awakening and returning to his usual mythic, rivalrous claim. Hypnosis also imposes at point N' the anteriority of H's desire and shows how self h is gradually produced by desire h; here, too, the process is in the present, but it demystifies the claims that have been made in the past.

By reestablishing the true chronology, revealing the mimetic reality of desire (at point N), and demystifying the mythic claim about the self (at N'), hypnosis brings scientific proof that should convince any open-minded observer about the mimetic reality of the interdividual relation. To the person hypnotized, it brings *recognition* of the mimetic mechanism and of the model as a model, rather than as an obstacle or a rival. It therefore brings healing, even if only temporarily, and even if the old mythic claims will soon revive again and return to pervert reality.

To understand hypnosis in this manner and "see" what actually happens in the inducing of the trance itself and in its therapeutic consequences, one must resolutely revise one's anthropology: one must abandon a psychology of the subject and not become polarized on individuals, but rather, grasping the mimetic nature of our desire, establish a psychology of relationship, of the interdividual relation, of the mutual influence of one subject on another. Every phenomenon of consciousness finds its origin in the other. And it is precisely because consciousness is otherness that it can be modified in and by the relation to the other, something that would otherwise be inexplicable. Léon Chertok rightly emphasized in this regard, in 1979, that "we are still the prisoners of Cartesian dualism," by an anthropology of *psyche* and *soma,* of soul and body.[28] Since that way of thinking about man is mythic, it is not surprising that it has undermined any previous effort to understand the psychological facts scientifically. The discovery of mirror neurons illumines this definitively.

In order to find a way out of this aporia, I have proposed substituting for the old Platonic and Cartesian anthropology a new anthropology founded on the psychological *reality* that I have tried to show, the reality of mimetic desire and of the *self-of-desire.*

The Mimetic Configurations of Neuroses and Psychoses

At point N', self h maintains itself in existence by forgetting that it is continuously being produced by desire h. Self h honestly thinks that desire h is its own, that it has produced it all by itself. Forgetting and misunderstanding are the simple psychological mechanisms by which self h manages to exist, along with its attributes: its memory, its consciousness, its language, and so on.

On the other hand, self h could also exist by way of a full and complete recognition of its filiation in relation to desire h, that it is the product of its own desire. The recognition of this would constitute a conversion that would permit the self to arrive at genuine wisdom. Such submission to reality is the characteristic of great sages and spiritual masters, but it is in principle available to everyone, if one is willing to understand and recognize the nature of one's desire and one's identity.

When one goes beyond the bounds of "normal" behavior (that is, behavior that identifies in a healthy manner with the other), one enters into the territory of neuroses and psychoses. In most cases, self h claims the ownership of its desire by putting in motion strategies that are *neurotic* (if it can still see the difference between itself and its model) or *psychotic* (if it can no longer see that difference), and it can pass back and forth from one of these states to the other depending on different events or parameters.

In the case of a neurotic structure, the self-of-desire *continues to see the difference* between itself and its model. When the model is seen as a rival, the desire-self will do everything it can to claim priority by proclaiming priority for "its" desire. Seen in this perspective, hysteria, for example, can be interpreted as a somatic representation of the other as rival, a representation that enables the neurotic both to deny the other and to vanquish him at the same time by submitting him symbolically to the hysterically manifested illness. To mask the mimetic reality of his desire, the hysteric symbolically represents the rival otherness in a circumscribed portion of his own body, such as a paralyzed limb, both denying the otherness of the other and vanquishing him (subjecting the other to the illness of paralysis so as to conquer him, while at the same time rendering him responsible for the disorder). This paralysis thus manifests the blockage of the relation. When the model is seen as an obstacle, the strategies employed tend to be those of obsessional neurosis or psychasthenia (anxiety, phobias, inhibitions, neurasthenia). In this configuration, the self-of-desire sees only too well the difference between itself and its model. And that difference seems to it insurmountable. For this reason it feels inhibited and constantly blocked by its model and becomes obsessed by it, which signifies feeling besieged by the model.

In the case of a psychotic structure, the self-of-desire *no longer sees the difference* between itself and its model. The model becomes for the self what Girard has called a "double."[29] There is then an abiding confusion between the self and the other. Psychotic discourse expresses the same kind of claim to the priority of its desire, but this time it does so in the mode of delirium. The story it tells of itself is delirious, because in this case the self and the other are constantly interchangeable. Here too, the clinical picture differs according to the status of the model: when the desire-self confuses itself with a model taken simply as *model,* it sees itself as brilliant and great. It takes itself for Napoleon or Jesus Christ. This sort of mimetic attitude produces paraphrenic psychoses (that is, ones involving prominent paranoid or other delusional symptoms), such as fantastic or cosmic deliria or delusions of grandeur. When the desire-self confuses itself with a model seen as an obstacle, it expels itself in a certain manner and enters into schizophrenia. It becomes at war with itself. The desire-self forbids itself, even before there has been any objective or exterior forbidding, and denies its own right to be.

When the self-of-desire confuses itself with a model it interprets as a rival, it enters into a merciless battle against itself. We then have all sorts of chronic, nonschizophrenic psychoses. The confusion between self and other will appear quite certain in the psychotic discourse: the self will accuse the other or others of persecuting it. To support its version of the facts, it will alienate a portion of its own sensations and perceptions in order to attribute them to the other; it will begin to hallucinate. Opposing its rival, its desire will maintain its essential claim to priority. This claim will show up in everything the hallucinatory patient says: "I am being followed. The other or the others are following me." It will say deliriously, but logically, "I preceded it, or them." Or in other words, "My desire is the original one, that of the other or others is a copy." That fundamental assertion is the heart of the problem. It can take an infinite variety of forms, and each delirious story will be different.

At point N, desire h claims its own anteriority, its precedence before the Desire H that inspired it, produced it, and aroused it, and of which it is a copy. Here too, in the best, most physiological of cases, the misunderstanding is founded on forgetfulness, and self h makes its claim to "its" desire in good faith.

Desire h could, on the other hand, submit to reality and accept the anteriority of Desire H and recognize that it has modeled itself on it. This attitude would permit it to accede to various degrees of realization and therefore to a measure of wisdom.

Between these two polar extremes, most examples of desire h frantically lay claim to their own anteriority in relation to Desire H in the neurotic mode (in which the desire-self sees the difference between itself and its model, as explained above) or in the psychotic mode (in which the desire-self no longer sees the difference between itself and its model), with various nuances running gradually between the one and the other extreme.

Interdividual psychology enables us to distinguish two nodal points, N and N', which are present in the psychology of all human beings and express two universal claims:

- At point N': the self claims ownership of its desire.
- At point N: the desire claims its own anteriority in relation to the Desire of the other that has served as its model.

In the case of any patient, in any course of psychotherapy, it will therefore be possible to analyze the situation at N and at N', and to try to determine what strategies the patient is using at these two points to make his claims and thereby to maintain his self in existence. This will enable us to draw the psychotherapy little by little into the domain of science, while also allowing us to better understand the unique character of each psychism, that is, of each self and of each desire as they adopt particular strategies for accomplishing their claim.

The misunderstanding on the part of the patient of the otherness of his or her desire makes the model into an obstacle or a rival, as we have seen. This is why, on the clinical level, rivalry is always an expression of an *illness of desire* and of a desire that has become fixated on a problematic model. To the extent that the patient does not recognize the otherness that runs through him, and to the extent that he tries, rather, to claim autonomy for his own being, he will persist in making his model into an adversary against whom he will ceaselessly oppose himself and whom he will tirelessly seek to dominate. This is even truer of romantic relationships, threatened as they are at every moment by the twists and turns of mimetic desire, which can tear a couple apart. Interdividual psychotherapy therefore has the task of *liberating patients from the rivalrous intensity that binds them passionately to their models or their partners* and quite often imprisons them in a relationship that is stuck.

Towards a New Clinical Anthropology

At this point in our inquiries and investigations, the reader would probably like to see a tentative schematization of the way human beings function as observed in clinical practice, but also in politics, in economic affairs, and in all domains of human activity.

In the light of what we now know, one may think of the brain as made up of three major components: a *cerebral cortex,* the seat of motor, sensitive, and cognitive activities; a *limbic system,* the seat of emotions, sensations, feelings, and mood; and, as we have also recently come to know, a system of *mirror neurons* that runs through each of the other two components.

> Because the limbic system interacts with the prefrontal lobes, there is an intimate relationship between our feelings (mediated by the emotional brain) and our thoughts (mediated by the cognitive brain). As a result, we (1) react emotionally to things we consciously understand to be happening, and (2) are consciously aware of the emotional richness of our lives. Communication between the cerebral cortex and limbic system explains why emotions sometimes override logic and, conversely, why reason can stop us from expressing our emotions in inappropriate situations.[30]

The mirror neuron system assures the cohesion of human beings with each other (and to some degree with certain animal species). This system makes communication possible, putting people on "the same wave length," through the empathy it establishes between them. And above all, this mirroring system guarantees the contagiousness of desire and desires by making them pass continually from one human being to another: mimetic desire passes from A to B and from B to A through the interplay of the imitation-suggestion vectors, which itself speeds up as rivalry exacerbates it to the point that the object becomes lost from sight in favor of attention that is directed exclusively toward the rivalry itself and toward the rival, who becomes "the unique object of my resentment." This mimetic rivalry will mobilize the attention of the protagonists, and with it, an increasingly large number of mirror neurons in all regions of the brain.

The mimetic marshalling of desire by the play of mirror neurons is automatic and inevitable, as we have seen. The mimetic escalation of rivalry also is ineluctable. The victim of these mechanisms that operate beyond its control, the brain will nevertheless try to integrate them. The mimetic and mechanical activity of the mirror neurons will reverberate through the other two major cerebral components:

—In the limbic system: rivalrous desire and mimetic rivalry will clothe themselves with sentiments and emotions. The particular attire chosen for this will differ according to culture, personalities, and circumstances. The sentiments may be those of love or hatred or resentment. The emotions may be of exaltation, of enthusiasm, of tears of joy or of distress, or of nervous fits, and so on. One's mood will also be affected and take the form of euphoria or of depression. And finally the body, too, will be drawn into expressing itself in all sorts of functional symptoms or, to an even greater degree, psychosomatic symptoms.

—In the cortical system: mimetic rivalry will adorn itself with moral and ethical judgments. My desire is the good, I am executing the will of God, my battle is sacred and blessed. My adversary, on the other hand, minion of Satan that he is, a servant of the devil, is the expression of evil and must be destroyed. Mirroring these attitudes, my adversary, on his side, will hold the same views and pronounce the same condemnations.

In this way, human beings are drawn unwittingly into mimetic rivalries that may be either private or public, individual or collective, and that engender various degrees of violence. At each point, the limbic brain will provide the emotional accompaniment, and the cortical brain will provide the ethical, moral, economic, and rational justification.

Let us sum all this up in a diagram:

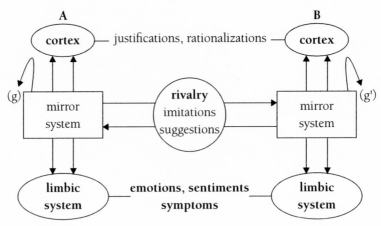

Figure 10

One sees in this diagram how the mirroring system, as it reverberates within the cortex, finds for "its" desire moral justifications that assimilate it to the divine, so that it produces g and g', that is, the *god-of-desire* and the *god-of-desire'*.

In the political sphere, A and B use these sorts of ethical and moral justification to make war on each other. Let us note how sometimes the one and the other will not hesitate to invoke the support of God and to claim to be instruments of the divine will. But these are gods with a small "g," gods in a mirror, mimetic gods. The protagonists are incapable of seeing that their little gods are subjective and identical, copied the one from the other. God with a capital "G" can only be one and is situated well above these conflicts and outside the diagram.

The Clinical Analysis of Rivalry

1. The Logic of Reciprocity

People are always reluctant to attribute intelligence to others, except when the other happens to be an enemy.

—*Einstein*

The two nodal points N and N', that were identified in our inquiry into theoretical psychopathology do not offer themselves to be seen distinctly as such in a clinical setting. Their clinical expression is usually simultaneous, with the subject laying claim at the same time to both his ownership (N') of his desire and its anteriority (N) in relation to the other's desire.

To speak of "laying a claim" is to speak of rivalry. This is the case each time the model in the interdividual relation becomes cast in the role of rival or obstacle.

Sometimes, however, the model remains a model and does not become a rival. Educational relationships and apprenticeships normally illustrate this. Learning to read, to speak, to write, to hunt, to eat, and so on, takes place by copying with increasing precision what a teacher teaches and shows.

On the clinical level, the prototypical form of an interdividual relation in which the model remains simply a model is the hypnotic rapport. In such a relationship, the subject recognizes the mimetic origin of his desire but

forgets it under the influence of the hypnotist, in proportion as the hypnotist's desire, having made the desire-self of the hypnotized subject fade away,
brings gradually into existence a new self, an *other-self-of-the-other-desire* (the
desire, that is, of the hypnotist).

Misunderstanding and Pathological Memories of Otherness

In hypnosis, it is clear that recognition of the otherness of the desire that animates the self can take the form of complete forgetfulness of the origin of that
desire. This is particularly evident in the case of posthypnotic suggestions
(actions suggested during the hypnotic session but commanded to take place
after the subject has awakened from it). We might recall here the patient of
Pierre Janet who, during the course of a hypnotic session, received a posthypnotic suggestion instructing him to open an umbrella in his classroom at the
university the next day. To his own surprise and that of the professor and the
other students, the poor fellow did that right in the middle of a class. When
the professor asked him sternly why he did it, he was completely oblivious as
to where his desire to do it, suggested by Janet, had come from. He mumbled
an excuse, saying something about how one can never be too careful about
when it might rain.

Such forgetfulness is not, however, a necessary condition for a peaceful interdividual relation. One can see examples of more or less complete remembrance
of the otherness of one's own desire in advanced initiates of possession cults
(such as Malkam Ayyahu, as described by Michel Leiris, which I analyzed
in some detail in *The Puppet of Desire*).[1] When the model remains simply a
model, the more extensive can be the remembrance, and the more advanced
the wisdom with respect to it.

Misunderstanding by the subject of the otherness of "his" or "her" desire
and of its mimetic nature is the same thing as claiming ownership of it and
claiming the anteriority of one's own desire in relation to that of the other.
Such misunderstanding amounts to *denial* rather than merely forgetfulness,
and it turns the model into a rival or an obstacle. When this happens, any
remembering of the otherness of his or her "own" desire will produce suffering in the subject and pathological symptoms.

When the classic studies of hysteria said that the hysteric "suffers from
memories," it was only the plural that was incorrect: it is a single, unique
memory, always the same one essentially—the memory that brings back
to the subject an awareness of the otherness of "his own" desire. It is this

memory that, without realizing it, those studies were alluding to. Hysteria is one particular mode of misunderstanding of the interdividual relation and of the mimetic nature of desire. It corresponds to a particular form of mimetic conflict. Hysterical desire tries always to deny the desire of the other, to affirm the anteriority and precedence of its own over that of the other. As was mentioned in the preceding chapter, when a hysteric "somatizes" conflict in a part of his own body, perhaps to the point of paralysis, he is manifesting the impossibility of a peaceful identification with the other, the impossibility of renouncing his pretensions regarding what he consider to be "his" desire. Anything that recalls to him the source of his desire and its model will trigger feelings of rivalry, and with it, his pathology. Whenever the model is a rival or an obstacle, the reminiscence is both powerful and frustrating, and the symptoms are dramatic.

As I also explained in *The Puppet of Desire,* the hysterical claim frequently expresses itself in competitive outbidding and emulation.[2] Pierre Briquet, writing in 1859, offered a clear example of hysterical emulation:

> It is through the effect of an impression made on the imagination that one can best explain the leaps and extraordinary postures of hysterics as well as the amazing feats they perform at the moment of their convulsive attack. In the presence of a girl undergoing convulsions, it is enough just to talk about another girl who has had extraordinary convulsions . . . to touch off in her in turn, and without her even being conscious of having been struck by that sight or that story and of becoming *aroused to emulation by it,* equally remarkable convulsions, and *even more extraordinary ones* than those that have served her as a *model.*[3]

The emulation and attempt to outdo the model here are obvious. The fundamental mechanism underlying these efforts can be described as a *mimetic hypertrophy,* in the sense of an extreme sensitivity to suggestion. Such heightened mimetic sensitivity is precisely what is denoted by the term *suggestibility.* Conversely, the mimetic counterpart of suggestion in the subject could properly be called "imitativity," but in practice we usually speak of it as influence or hypnosis.

The status of the model—whether it is simply a model, or a rival, or an obstacle—will not of itself produce the same clinical expression. The form the clinical expression takes will depend on whether the mimesis bears essentially on the appearance of the model, on his being, or on his desire.

Imitation That Bears on Appearance

When the model remains simply a model, the imitation, as was said, takes the character of apprenticeship. The pupil copies what the teacher says, does, or shows him. The pupil may copy the model's gestures, his dress, his verbal expressions, his accent, and so on. From kindergarten to the university, one can observe these sorts of mimetic attitudes, which establish fashions among adolescents, for example, or allow one to distinguish a member of one student group from that of another.

When the model becomes a rival, the imitation may take the form of aping, mockery, or caricature. It can be aggressive, or as in the case of the music hall or of *Saturday Night Live,* it can be playful. Imitations of this sort win adherence or laughter by reproducing the model in some witty manner.

When the model is too powerful or exalted an obstacle, imitation is impossible. The model in this case is too perfect—so perfect that he renders helpless the pupil or the admirer, who feels himself impotent, deprived of value, depressed, and forced to give up any attempt to imitate. The bitterness and resentment this gives rise to can lead to clinical depression.

A girl who dreams of becoming a "supermodel" may know that she will never be able to attain the ideal physique that would require. If she becomes polarized on that ideal image, she can become depressed and increasingly discouraged ("I'll never make it"), sinking into real despair. She will know that she can never equal such a woman, that her model ideal is unattainable, that she finds herself in an impossible situation. Some forms of anorexia or bulimia certainly express discouragement of that sort. Anorexics want to punish their bodies by depriving them of nourishment; bulimics, on the other hand, fatten their bodies by gorging and deforming them, in order to appease their anguish by pathologically distancing themselves from their models.

Imitation That Bears on What the Model Has

When the model remains simply a model—something that does not often actually happen—this may inspire in the subject an effort to get for himself something the model has. It is possible that in such an act of appropriation the subject may manage to differentiate himself from the model by, for example, working for a long time in order to be able to pay for a car like his model's.

Or the mimesis of appropriation may turn the model into a rival. Then it will be the particular object the rival is trying to get for himself that one will want to acquire, or something the rival has and is trying to keep for himself.

This sort of situation, as was mentioned earlier, evolves in the direction of mimetic conflict and increasing violence. I also said that at the high point of such mimetic conflict, where the violence becomes most intense, the object tends to be lost sight of by the combatants in favor of their passion for rivalry as such, so that they founder under the waves of rivalrous passion.

Interdividual psychology has sometimes been reproached for not taking sufficient account of the object, even for hiding it or spiriting it away.[4] But it is not we who hide the object, but rather the rival combatants who become absorbed in their fight to the death to such a degree that they lose sight of it. There are even situations in which there seems to be no actual object of rivalry, a matter to which I will return further on.

When the model becomes an obstacle, it appears to reserve invincibly for itself what it has. The model's disciple always feels pervaded by the idea that he will never succeed in getting what the model has, even if, in some paranoid cases, he may already possess it. Othello possesses his wife Desdemona, and she loves him. But his paranoia makes him feel that he does not possess her, that she belongs to another. Since the rival is not at hand, he adopts the approach of the evil mother in the judgment of Solomon: he kills Desdemona so as to deny her to a rival who never existed except in the delirium of his mimetic pathology.

Here we have an excellent clinical example of mimetic psychopathology. All the forms of paranoia seem to me to arise from the sort of mimetic configuration in which the model is deliriously perceived as an insuperable obstacle to the appropriation of an object and the satisfaction of desire. Other pathologies can also develop out of that same pattern of misinterpretation, especially depressive pathologies, which can tend toward despair and even suicide.

Some people, when they understand that they will never be able to "have" some desired object, or that it is irretrievably lost to them, will sink into a deep depression. A man who has been openly deceived, manipulated, and abandoned may start thinking about suicide. He believes that he is *worth* nothing, because he *is* nothing. The "self" that was constituted in the relation to the other has been completely wiped out. This is why he can have the feeling that his life is over, that he will never be able to love again. His mourning for this can be extremely painful. This is doubtless why one never completely gets over a separation: to get over it would mean having to resuscitate that "self." But that self could be reborn only in the presence of the departed loved one.

Desire to Imitate the Model's Being

When the model remains simply a model, the form of mimesis that seeks to imitate the model's being becomes identification. When the model is just a model, identification is a normal mechanism for avoiding violence. By identifying with his or her model, the disciple becomes the model in a certain manner and takes nonviolent possession of him.

One can see clearly how this mechanism works in the phenomena of what is called adorcism. Adorcism, a term coined by cultural anthropologists to refer to the type of spirit possession practiced in a culturally approved way in Africa, represents the opposite of exorcism. Exorcism is the effort to drive out (through prayer, rites, magic, etc.) alien spirits that have invaded and taken possession of a person. Adorcism refers to an effort to invoke or conjure in such spirits. This is a widespread religious practice in parts of Africa, but it also has counterparts all over the world—as in the case of traditional Siberian, Korean, Eskimo, or other shamans, and also among modern Western spirit mediums. I will not go into exorcism and adorcism in detail here, since I devoted an entire chapter to each of these topics in *The Puppet of Desire,* but I will summarize a few of the main points regarding adorcism in particular, since it is a good illustration of the sort of benign mimetic identification that I think is important to understand in the present context as well.[5]

Adorcism is a version of what René Girard termed "external mediation," as described above in chapter 1: this is a case in which the mediator (the model) is not operating within one's own sphere of activity, so that he cannot be a competitor; he is, in that sense, "external" to one's actual world of potential conflict. Amadis of Gaul, as was mentioned earlier, represented an ideal to Don Quixote, not someone he might compete with. Jesus is similarly an "external" mediator for a Christian; the Christian seeks to "dwell in" Christ and prays that Christ may "dwell in" him or her for the enhancement of his or her being, but the Christian does not see Jesus as a potential rival. To a Christian believer, that very idea would seem so absurd as to be virtually inconceivable. This, rather, is what can be described as a "vertical" relationship, as compared with the "horizontal" relationship one would have with someone whose goods or whose being one might envy and seek to take away or outdo.

In the case of adorcistic possession cults, what is sought is that a god, genie, spirit, or other culturally defined higher entity, the culturally idealized Other, might "take possession of" or "incarnate" himself or itself in a receptive subject, for the benefit not only of that subject but also for that of the subject's community. When the rite of adorcism is successful, the possessed subject then becomes identified with the higher Other not only in his or her own mind but also in the minds of the members of the community and its religious authorities. The person possessed, then, is what I was referring to earlier as "an advanced initiate" when I spoke of Malkam Ayyahu. Not everyone is susceptible to such spirit-possession, and those who are good at it are highly valued within the cultures that are organized around these phenomena. As Michel Leiris says, "The person who is advanced in possession not only plays a healing role, but may also be consulted as a soothsayer, an arbiter, a director of consciences, or a counselor."[6]

Leiris's description of Malkam Ayyahu can serve to illustrate the structure of a healthful identification as it takes place in adorcism:

> For each activity of his life . . . [the advanced initiate] has a particular *zâr* in charge of that activity. This happens to such a degree that his real personality may completely disappear, so that a woman like Malkam Ayyahu, for example, who is permanently possessed by a genie, even without a trance, no longer speaks of herself except in the third person, the way a *zâr* speaks of his "horse." After I had observed the life of Malkam Ayyahu for several months, I came to the conclusion that her *zârs* became for her a sort of wardrobe of personalities that she could put on according to need or as fitted the circumstances of her daily existence, personalities that made available ready-made attitudes and patterns of behavior, in a manner halfway between actual life and theater.[7]

We see that in her possessed state, Malkam Ayyahu always *speaks of herself in the third person.* By doing so, she confirms the psychological and anthropological analysis I have been developing. By using this grammatical construction, she signifies that (1) it is desire that is the subject of the discourse, desire who is speaking, and (2) it is the energy and action of desire itself that constitutes what we call the "self." Only a new anthropology that shows how the self develops and generates itself continuously as a desire-self can make it clear that the subject of the discourse is desire itself and that the subject of the action is the self produced or generated by that same desire. The desire that does this is mimetic; it is copied from, modeled on, inspired by the other's desire. Malkam Ayyahu recognizes explicitly the otherness in each of her desires, the mimetic origin of each of her psychological motivations. She *gives them names* and *represents* them. On this level of initiatory wisdom, it is as much a matter of manifesting *inspiration* as it is of living a *possession.*

She enacts her role as an advanced initiate by continuously manifesting her submission to the interdividual relation, her inspiration by the other, and her recognition of the mimetic character of desire.

This is what she constantly demonstrates by returning to her "wardrobe of personalities" to change her zâr every time her desire changes. She does this by using gestures and mannerisms that are identifiable by those around her as those of that particular zâr in order to emphasize that the source of each of her psychological movements is that *other*. The best proof that she is not simply playing a role and that she is representing not simply the other but the *desire* of the other is that she speaks of herself in this way in the third person. It is desire that is the real subject, the speaker, of her discourse, while the "self" remains the subject of her action.

One also sees cases of possession in Western clinical settings, and these are often clearly pathogenic. There are cases, for example, in which patients may undergo a nervous crisis or depression or adopt an aggressive attitude, and then eventually come to realize that in those moments, they were reproducing the behavior of their father or mother, who "possessed" them temporarily due to an excess of identification triggered by some particular set of circumstances.

Most of the time, however, identification functions as a constructive process that, as Freud also argued, is fundamental for psychological development and the formation of the personality. Identification, when it remains benign, is the most effective mechanism for avoiding rivalry with one's models. It serves as a process by which one can construct one's self through one's models in a peaceful manner. During the course of an individual's life, such identifications are many, constituting what one might call the "patchwork" of the personality.

When benign identification becomes impossible and the model becomes a rival, the being of the subject can come to feel as if it is at risk, as if the subject's very existence is threatened. This mimetic configuration can engender murderous violence that is often blind and undifferentiated, and it seeks to discharge itself on all sorts of substitutes. Lynch mobs and rioters who put scapegoats to death are the playthings of such a mimetic eruption. Serial killers should probably also be included in this category. Their undifferentiated violence multiplies itself in such sequences of murder in a culture that is no longer effectively held back from violence by rites and prohibitions. A serial killer, one might say, tries to kill the crowd, while in a lynching, the crowd kills an individual. The person lynched stands alone before the lynch mob, whose members, caught up in a single collective movement of violence, all become identical. The serial killer stands alone in face of the crowd of victims, who seem to him all similar and interchangeable. His own model-rival is the whole world, every "other," and if he could, he would kill all of humanity—most especially those who are the objects of his desires (young women, brunettes, prostitutes, children, and so on).

When the model is an obstacle, the subject's existence finds itself before an aporia. His or her personality finds itself in a situation in which it is absolutely impossible for it to develop. In a clinical setting one finds this in autism. If it should be proven that autistics have a deficit of mirror neurons, which in itself would prevent them from identifying with and imitating a model, then every model will be an obstacle from the very start of that person's life. Clinically, we also find schizophrenics—split, discordant, fragmented personalities—who are unable to put themselves together, because their model is an obstacle to their existence.

Imitation of Desire

When the model remains simply a model for the disciple, a peaceful and beneficent interdividual relation can take shape, made up of confidence, love, and constructive dynamism. This is the case when a mother's desire serves as a positive inspiration for her child's desire, and such a source of inspiration and energy can remain effective throughout one's life. The same can happen in the case of a father's desire, and all the more when the desires of both the father and the mother unite in the same direction.

In psychopathology, one can also observe this type of configuration in some forms of paraphrenia, in which the patient becomes persuaded, in some corner of his psyche, that he is the descendant of some great personage and, without anyone knowing it, models his life and his actions in accord with the real or supposed desire of that personage. The delirium in such a case need not interfere with the person's daily activity, and one would then say that it has been encysted.

When the model becomes a rival, on the other hand, two desires enter into competition or into conflict. Among clinical cases, there are several kinds that illustrate that pattern, such as cases of diabolic possession, which was very common in our own culture in the sixteenth and seventeenth centuries and which one can still observe today in some places. In *The Puppet of Desire,* I explained in detail how hysteria is a clinical expression of that sort of rivalry: there, mimetic conflict gets represented somatically as the hysteric attempts to isolate the otherness outside the self in a bodily part and to dominate it.[8] The hysterical symptom mimics the rival relationship and symbolizes it—the better to mask and hide it. We also see, in the clinical setting, a psychopathology of couples that expresses the rivalry between two indissociable desires: the jealousy of the other half of the couple, which I will analyze in detail in the next section of this chapter. I often say to my patients who are caught in that sort of rivalry that if it is difficult to separate from one's best friend, it is even more difficult to renounce one's best enemy.

When the model is an obstacle, when the model's desire systematically obstructs that of the disciple, the clinical expression takes the form of phobias and obsessions. In the case of phobias, the desire either avoids or tries to drive away the obstacle, or else flees from it. If it meets it head on, it is seized with anguish.

In cases of obsession, on the other hand, the desire keeps returning, obsessively and compulsively, to rub up against the obstacle. It goes over and over lost battles, so that the wall constituted by the desire-obstacle becomes its "wailing wall." I said to a patient once that he had fallen into a "Waterloo syndrome," as if he were Napoleon replaying endlessly and compulsively his lost battle, going over all sorts of "ifs": "If only Grouchy had brought up his troops. . . ." He cannot think about any other battle, even though setting up the same scene again and again with the same events will always lead inexorably to the same defeat.

Rivalry, the Clinical Expression of Mimetic Desire

The different phenomena that we have just gone over show mimetic desire in action. Invisible and constantly denied, it reveals itself through its effects: its capacity to infiltrate itself into the other, to animate him, to transmit psychological movement to him. The more aggravated mimetic rivalry becomes, the sicker becomes desire. Many of our sufferings today are really illnesses of desire. I have offered some examples, and my practice brings me new ones every day.

How can one prevent, contain, or disarm such rivalry? If one reads the story of the Garden of Eden against the grain of the common interpretation, it looks as if the prohibition was a fundamental protection against mimetic rivalry. Prohibition is also important in psychology for the process of educating desire so that it can learn ways to avoid rivalry. But since the time when it became "forbidden to forbid," many parents seem to have forgotten how needed is this essential gift for their children. Without the experience of prohibition, desire cannot take hold of itself and learn to control its rivalry.

Pathologies of desire proliferate in the modern world: delinquency, gratuitous violence, pedophilia, drugs, chaotic innovations of all sorts that serve only to manifest the rivalrous passion that they excite everywhere and in everyone at the points N (at which the self claims anteriority for its desire) and N' (where it claims ownership of its desire), as shown in figure 9 and explained in the preceding chapter. The subject asserts more and more vehemently his claim to ownership of "his" desire without even really knowing what he wants, that is, what is the truth of his desire. Desire, for its part, frantically asserts its anteriority, that it desired the object before the other did and that it therefore has a prior claim to it. But the infinite multiplication of rival desires ends up with desire getting lost in the madness of universal and incessant grasping.

The Ten Commandments were brought down the mountain by Moses. All of them prohibited and condemned mimetic rivalry, whether by positively prescribing the love of God and of one's parents, or by forbidding the consequences of rivalry: "Thou shalt not kill." The last of the commandments, against covetousness, as I emphasized in chapter 2, specifically forbids all forms of mimetic rivalry.

Christ declared that he had come to confirm and fulfill the Law, not to set it aside. He simply gave his hearers the key to the Kingdom of God: love. Love makes disobedience of the Ten Commandments impossible; it makes their observance natural. In the logic of love, if you "love your neighbor as yourself," the Ten Commandments follow of themselves.

God did not judge Adam and Eve: He simply drew conclusions from their conduct and allowed the future consequences of their action to unfold. The first of those consequences was that they suddenly found themselves out of the earthly paradise. The message of Christ concludes the age-long history of the Bible and of the Jewish people: the earthly paradise, the Garden of Eden, and the Kingdom of God are all one and the same. They represent a time and a place where mimetic rivalry and false differences are safely shut away in a forbidden tree and do not pollute the trees, the plants, the flowers, the animals, and the human beings around them. The path by which to return there and the key to enter have but a single name: love.

Love is, of course, the goal we wish to attain, but how are we to do that? Love is a sentiment, and in our ordinary psychological experience, sentiments, it is said, "cannot be commanded." It is here that the mimetic theory can offer us precious help.

In a disciple-model relationship in which the model remains simply a model, everything that the model gives or teaches is immediately taken up, integrated, and indeed loved by the disciple. The love Adam felt for the woman God gave him is an example. Love is a sentiment that colors a peaceful interdividual relationship in which the model remains a model.

In an interdividual relationship in which the model becomes a rival or an obstacle, on the other hand, the sentiment tends toward hatred. Upstream from mimetic rivalry, rivalrous desire colors relationships with sentiments such as envy, jealousy, resentment, bitterness, and so on. Downstream from it, that is, once mimetic conflict has broken out, rivalry colors relationships with feelings of hatred and detestation that can even lead to a desire to kill.

It is clear that sentiments are only colorations that the interdividual relation takes on as a function of the workings of the mechanism that transforms the model into a rival or an obstacle. This fact is a basis for hope, because a mimetic psychotherapy, which aims at enabling recognition of the mechanisms we have described, can disengage those hatreds and resentments and open the path that, exiting from rivalrous misunderstanding, leads to love.

I have reviewed the different modes of universal mimesis as they bear upon appearance, having, being, and finally on desire itself. With regard to each of these, I have tried to show that their clinical expression will differ according to the way in which, within the interdividual relation, the model either remains a model or becomes a rival or obstacle. This schematization has had a didactic purpose, to simplify for the sake of clarity. It is clear that in clinical reality all these patterns often become mixed together; mimesis can bear *simultaneously* on the appearance, the possessions, the being, and the desire of the model. It is also evident that, in the evolution of clinical cases, the model in the interdividual relation tends to evolve from model to either rival or obstacle. In psychotherapy, what one hopes for is that the evolution might move the model back from being a rival or obstacle to being simply a model again.

Very often, the task of psychotherapy will be to try to prevent rivals and obstacles from regularly being taken as models, which is what psychoanalysts appropriately call the "repetition syndrome." It happens frequently in our world that rivalry as such becomes our model, locking the patient into a series of rivalries and rendering him unable to form an interdividual relationship that is not rivalrous. The many who rush to take an obstacle as their model develop many rationalizations for it: he is in my way, he is hiding an object from me, or forbidding it—*that,* therefore, is what I desire! It is only with great difficulty that one can manage to "unhook" them from that quest for the impossible.

Thus it may be said that the ultimate goal of all psychotherapy is to lead the patient to wisdom and thence to happiness. But what is wisdom in the perspective we are developing here? It is to learn to *desire what one has.* It is also to learn to *protect love,* which will always be threatened by rivalry.

To illustrate these points, we will examine some cases of couples in acute or chronic crisis and try to notice in each of them the intricate steps of mimetic desire and the snares of rivalry. We now know that in every couple's relationship, one is likely to find a mixture of desire and rivalry. Desire is rivalrous, and rivalry is desiring. It is a matter, therefore, of trying carefully to "pluck out" the rivalry, to disentangle it from desire, and yet do this without impairing or weakening the desire—a difficult and risky undertaking.

I think that in a clinical perspective one can, in a general and schematic manner, distinguish two forms of jealousy that threaten couples: (1) jealousy of a third party—when some other person, a lover or mistress, comes to threaten the cohesion of the couple; (2) jealousy of the other partner—when the couple is gnawed at from within by rivalry, envy, jealousy, or resentment. These phenomena, which can insinuate themselves into the relationship of any two lovers or spouses, will be the same whether the couple is homosexual or heterosexual.

In this latter type of jealousy, which I like to call "jealousy of one's other half," the potency of the rivalry in an interdividual relationship outweighs by far the potency of desire in it. It is that variety of jealousy that we will inquire into first.

2. JEALOUSY BETWEEN THE MEMBERS OF A COUPLE

Never trust couples who hold hands: if they won't let go of each other, it's because they're afraid they might kill each other.

—*Groucho Marx*

Jealousy regarding one's partner is particularly dreadful and devastating for couples: the rival in this case is not someone outside the relationship but one of its two members. Gnawed at in this way by mimetic rivalry, the couple finds itself in a constant struggle over power, one seeking to dominate the other. This variety of mimetic relation clothes and colors itself with new sentiments: rancor, claiming of rights, anger, depression, resentment. It also adorns itself with moral and intellectual justifications: efficiency, power, the pursuit of happiness, the interest of the children, economic interests, and so on. Reproaches and arguments about intentions flow in torrents. Rivalry gradually consumes both desire and the interdividual relation. In some cases, it intensifies to the point of becoming a passion capable of leading to the worst excesses and disasters.

The Infernal Seesaw

Couples that are bound by jealousy of each other are always prisoners of the same mechanism: their mirroring desires continually oscillate between the positions of dominating or being dominated—the pattern of relation that transactional analysis calls "one up" and "one down." The couples may be married couples, or they may be two men or two women, or professional couples, or associates. The jealousy will establish an endless power struggle between the partners: each one will rise or fall in proportion as the other falls or rises, as if they were facing each other from opposite ends of a seesaw, or as if the one and the other were no more than head and tail of the same coin. If one is up, the other has to be down, and vice versa. For one to stand out, the other must be driven back into the shadows; for one to rise, the other must be beaten down. Raymond Devos has described this conflictual interdependence perfectly in one of his sketches:

> My right foot is jealous of my left foot. When one advances, the other wants
> to get ahead of it. And I, fool that I am, go for a walk!

That walk may not only lead us quite far down the destructive path of rivalry, it may also tempt us to accelerate until without realizing it, we are running toward a precipice.

We can represent these situations by the image of a seesaw, like those one sees in children's playgrounds: a plank moving up and down on each side of a stationary support, with the game for the children seated at each end consisting of going up and down alternately, as in this diagram:

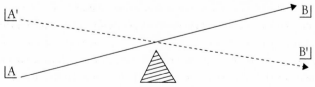

Figure 11

Here the interdividual relation is represented by the plank itself. One can understand immediately that the two protagonists, A and B, can never "win," that is, "rise" together: if one goes up, the other must as a consequence go down, and to the same degree. Desire A is here in rivalry with desire B. The two desires are identical: to dominate, to have power, to get the upper hand, to be "one up." To get higher than the other, A can try either to rise higher himself or to force B lower. It is the second solution that is more commonly adopted by A and is therefore the most frequently encountered in clinical practice.

One might observe, for example, a couple who appear so close that they cannot get along without each other. But in reality the couple is suffering and in a constant state of crisis: one of the partners never ceases to put the other down, to criticize him or her while pretending to defend or counsel her, let us say, "for her own good." Aggressiveness often masks itself with good intentions and feelings. The aggressive partner will put his partner in check at every step she takes by setting goals for her that are beyond her reach, while demanding a contrary attitude from her toward himself.

This kind of rivalry can also infiltrate a couple's sexual relationship: a grande dame of French society once declared at an elegant dinner, in her lover's presence: "Thank God I'm frigid! It saves me from having to submit to a man or let him get under my skin the way so many poor women do. This way I'm always free to choose my lovers and my husbands as suits my own interests." Thanks to that approach, she amassed an enormous fortune and escaped the famous "yearning" after her husband to which God condemned women, as we saw, in Genesis 3:16.

There are some women who resent it fiercely when men give them pleasure. They feel as if they have been conquered, that they have been proven weak, that they have allowed themselves to be possessed. "He had me, I yielded to him!" As one of my patients explained to me, "Men! I let them take pleasure as I please, but never myself." The day one of them succeeded in bringing her, against her will, to sexual climax, she had only one thought in mind: to regain the advantage and destroy him. When neither wants to climax before the other, the foreplay can prolong itself for hours until one of them, exhausted, finally gives up. Men who do not experience orgasm are usually men who either cannot or do not wish to surrender themselves and who feel that if they did so they would be letting themselves be conquered. They have no consciousness of the rivalry that deprives them of sexual fulfillment. At the opposite extreme, there are also men who tend to be so abject in their sexual relations that the moment they take their beloved into their arms, they become like slaves.

In this type of pathology, one can see that the rivalry seems to have no precise object. It is the desire to dominate alone, mimetic and identical in the two partners, that absorbs them and imprisons them. Sometimes interdividual psychopathology has been criticized for not giving its proper place to the object, but this type of pathology shows the extent to which mimetic rivalry can become self-feeding and bind the protagonists in perpetual conflict.

In this sort of case, psychotherapy must focus on showing the protagonists the reality of their situation, on making them conscious of their endless game of seesaw, so as to convince them both to get off the seesaw and establish a different kind of relationship. What one has to do, that is, is get them to change their game. This is often quite difficult, because they can get quite attached to the game, which fascinates them and inflames their passions, particularly when it gets hot and fast, so that it binds them together more intensely than love or any other sentiment, even if that intensity may prove destructive. The more rapidly the rivalry circulates between the two, the more the oscillations of the seesaw will speed up to the point that the rising and falling of A and B seem to coincide. Each of them will come little by little to see in the other a monstrous, terrifying double, a mixture of god and beast. This frightening perception is accompanied by hatred and fear. The partners in the couple will no longer recognize each other. They will develop the illusion that it is by more and more frantic swings of the seesaw that they can succeed in extricating themselves from the conflict and finally stabilizing the situation.

Let's return now to the case of Françoise, about whom we were talking before we began our long theoretical detour. Françoise drinks because Lucien deceives her, or Lucien deceives her because Françoise drinks—we see the seesaw at work. In the course of subsequent sessions, it seemed impossible to find a solution. Françoise said, "It's because he has a mistress that he neglects me and that I hate him." And her husband, for his part, declared, "It's because she drinks and then badgers me about my faults when she's drunk that I gradually came to neglect her and finally took a mistress."

I managed to get her husband gradually to realize that rivalry had been eating away at their marriage behind the surface justification: on his part, that it was a so-called "third party," alcohol, that was causing the problem, and on hers, that there was a *real* third party, as indeed there was, but one who was not the origin but the consequence of their rivalry, their jealousy of their other half.

I found out that in the beginning they both had the same profession. She was less talented than he was, and he was having greater success and winning more rapid advancement. Then they had two children and she stopped working, and she managed to drop the rivalry for a while. But as the children grew up and her husband advanced further in his career, Françoise fell into the infernal trap of rivalrous passion and found recourse in alcohol. At first she drank to console herself or "buck up her spirits," but then, seeing how her alcoholism was wounding her husband, she began to drink more and more.

Confronted with certain situations, a therapist has to recognize his powerlessness. In psychology, as in medicine, we sometimes encounter incurable patients. All I could do in this case was to explain to the husband the mechanism of their mimetic rivalry so as to help him better manage, and endure, their situation, and at any rate, not to make it worse.

Once a couple has got onto the seesaw, they seldom manage to get off it. More often they plunge into an increasing rivalry that will gradually destroy their relationship. To turn such a situation around means to suspend one's hostile gestures—that is, to slow down the rhythm of the swings of the seesaw—long enough to let the initial movement that gave birth to them come into view. And, as I said, what makes this especially difficult is that beneath the surface we often feel an attachment to the rivalrous games that bind us so intensely to one another.

What makes couples therapy very difficult is that there is no third party to expose other than the symbolic third party, which is the power that each lusts after. In most cases, if a couple comes to see me together and I expose their reciprocal rivalry, they quickly form a league against me in a fleeting reconciliation behind my back. A failed psychotherapy is one in which the therapist looked like the ideal scapegoat. I prefer to see the members of a couple separately so as to try to help each in turn to understand what is going on. Sometimes it is sufficient to set the relationship on a more pacific course if just one of the two can be brought to understand the mechanisms of which their marriage has become the plaything.

Let us return, now, to Françoise and her husband. The husband comes to me, and I challenge him: "Since you can no longer stand the alcoholism of your wife, why don't you divorce her?"

"I don't want to do that. My wife wouldn't survive it, and my children would be traumatized. I can't leave my wife all alone; who'd take care of her when she falls on the floor and put her to bed?"

"I understand. Your wife must have some sense of that too. That's how she's found a way to hold onto you—a regrettable way, certainly, but an effective one, since the alcohol may be what separated you from her but it's that too that prevents you from leaving her. I must tell you that alcoholism is a disease. Only your wife can take the initiative to take care of herself, get disintoxicated, and leave alcohol behind. If she doesn't do so, perhaps it is because she senses that it is only the alcohol that keeps you with her, because you can't let yourself surrender the field to that rival. The mechanism of rivalry can be so absurd that it is able to clothe itself with irreproachable sentiments, such as the fear of what might happen to her, and with morality: duty, devotion, and self-sacrifice for the sake of the children. All that is even true, and I can't advise you to make any different decision. On the other hand, I have a question for you: why don't you try to unblock the situation by leaving your mistress?

"It's my mistress that makes it possible for me to bear this situation. She understands me, she encourages me, she supports me. Without her, I don't know what I'd do."

"In sum, then, your wife drinks to keep you, and you keep your mistress in order to be able to stay with your wife."

"Yes, one can look at it that way," he says with a smile. "It takes a sense of humor to accept your way of seeing it."

"What I find remarkable is that between you and your wife there is nothing but rivalry and conflict, and yet that holds you together powerfully. Between you and your mistress, there is only desire, and that desire holds the two of you together just as powerfully. Why, between you and your mistress, is the desire so pure, so empty of all rivalry? Because that is constantly being unloaded onto a third party who stands always between you and whose constant exclusion cements your union. This excluded, sacrificial third party is your wife.

"That's an interesting idea, but it doesn't solve my problem!"

"Sometimes there are problems that can't be solved. Still, I think a clear perception of reality can never be useless. You could, for example, gradually improve the situation by drawing closer to your wife and trying to get her to join with you against the third party that separates you, alcohol. She will not give it up, but you could show her that you understand her, that you are both trapped, she by alcohol and you by your mistress, and that it might be possible for the two of you, perhaps, to exclude both of them, at least within the bosom of the family. Insist on the family tie, which is stronger than any other and has a just claim to take precedence. Claim that it is in the best interest of the children and then stopping making any reproaches about her alcoholism.

Don't even talk about it anymore; pretend you don't even notice it. And if she talks to you about your mistress, tell her it's ancient history, that you are no longer seeing her, that it is your family and your profession that you care about now and . . . try to be careful."

A few weeks later I saw Françoise again. She seemed to be feeling better. She said, "Nothing has been straightened out, but I can recognize that my husband is nicer, more thoughtful, and more patient."

"And are you still drinking just as much?"

"You're exaggerating. I never drank that much. I'm not an alcoholic. But it's true that lately I've felt less desire to drink."

"So much the better. I'm glad to hear it. Try to drink less, especially when your husband is around, and try to get closer to him. Talk to him about the children, make plans together. Give him attention in little ways that you haven't done in a long time. Maybe both of you will be less unhappy."

Sometimes even if they understand the underlying reality of mimetic desire and rivalry, even if they can see the triangles of husband-Françoise-alcohol or husband-Françoise-mistress, it is not possible to make the couple get off their seesaw. But they can, as I've tried to show, do something to slow down the swings of the seesaw and gradually efface the monstrous appearance conferred on the other by its frenetic oscillations, and thus to bring into view again the face of the person one loved.

I see two young people around forty years old come into my office, Paul and Suzanne. They are well dressed, confident, very "professional." After they sit down across from me, they look me over as if it were I who had come to them for consultation. I learn that they are attorneys in a large international law firm. They work in the same legal department and have been married seven years and have two children, a three-year-old and a five-year-old. Both have had brilliant professional success.

"What is the problem?"

"Our life has become a hell," they both answer together. "We can't stand each other, and yet we love each other. We argue about everything and anything. At the office we argue over who's going to get the most interesting cases, and if one of us makes a presentation that's well received by everyone else, only our partner criticizes us. At home it's even worse: we reproach each other about the dishes that need washing, the garbage that's not been taken out, the children not being bathed or put to bed, the meal not being ready yet, and so on. We have come to see you, against our better judgment, on the advice of a friend who knows you."

"Paul, what is it you love about Suzanne?"

Paul sits up and looks at his wife in a questioning manner. "I love everything about Suzanne, her looks, her style, her laugh, her intelligence, but I'm also suffering with good reason, because I hate her for not having confidence in me, even about little things."

"And you, Suzanne, what do you love about Paul?"

"He's an extraordinary fellow. We were students together, and we've been together ever since. He's the most intelligent man I know. But he seems to go out of his way to oppose me. We can't talk to each other without shouting. Whose fault do you think it is?"

"I'm not a judge, and you're not in court. It's nobody's fault; the fault lies in the situation. You do everything together, twenty-four hours a day, and since both of you are intelligent and competent, you both want to be the boss. This has set going a continuous rivalry between you that is poisoning your relationship."

"Do you have a solution?"

They look at me somewhat warily, and I can sense that they are feeling a temptation to conspire against me, to cast me out together and by doing so give themselves a few moments of respite and happiness.

It is in moments like this that the work of a psychiatrist and therapist becomes painful: one feels an anxiety connected both with the fear of being victimized and with the urgency of thinking of an answer, something to say that will reduce the tension. This can be difficult, and sometimes even impossible. In the present case, an idea comes to me: "Do you like games? Would you be willing to play a game?"

"Let's be serious," says Paul.

"I'm quite serious. I'd like to propose that you play the game of government."

"Explain what you mean," says Suzanne. "Because we don't have a lot of time."

"In a government, each minister has a precise set of responsibilities and powers and does not meddle in the departments of other ministers. In the case of certain very difficult questions, several departments can be involved and develop conflicts, and their respective ministers then look for arbitration to the prime minister or the president of the Republic."

"What does that have to do with us?"

"It looks to me as if the two of you have set up a government whose ministers each want to take charge of all the departments and all problems. That can't work, and the reason you've come to see me is that your government is on the verge of resigning."

"I see," says Suzanne. "Let's say that there might be some truth in what you are saying. What should we do?"

"Play at dividing up the ministries. Form, between the two of you, a coherent government in which the various tasks will be well defined and appropriately distributed. Let's begin with you, Suzanne: what ministries do you want?"

"What would you advise for me?"

That question from Suzanne encourages me and gives me the feeling she's starting to get into the game. "Traditionally," I say, "I think that in a couple, the wife directs the ministry of the Interior, as well as the ministries of Social Affairs and of Education. But you can adopt another approach and assign those functions to the man, if you like. The important thing is that you should both agree on them."

"How should we divide them?"

"If one of you takes charge of Social Affairs and Education, the other could be in charge of Finances, the Economy, and Foreign Affairs. He could manage the budget, handle the taxes, pay the bills, and take care of relations with colleagues and group management."

"And if we need arbitration," asks Suzanne, "who will be the prime minister?"

"That is a problem, all right. But in the case of such a small government, do you really need a prime minister? Couldn't arbitration just be worked out between the two ministers?"

"In any case," concludes Paul, "you've amused us, and we've had a good time. We'll give all this a little thought."

According to what I've heard, Paul and Suzanne are still together. Our mutual friend who sent them to me tells me that they still laugh when they think about the session we had, which they refer to as "exotic." They're about to leave for a vacation in the Caribbean and they seem to be looking forward to it. I tell myself, "Oh, I forgot to assign the ministry of Leisure and Tourism . . ."

A reader who has followed along with me this far will have understood what happened between Paul and Suzanne: they were on a seesaw playing at who was up and who was down, and that oscillating, undecidable rivalry was accelerating. My idea was to get them to organize their relationship within the framework of a different game so as to get them off of the infernal seesaw. And since they were high-powered corporate lawyers, I had to propose a game with roles that would seem flattering to them: so there they are, ministers!

The news about Fabienne was not as good. Let us recall that Fabienne had sacrificed her career in order to take care of her two children, who came to bore her increasingly, to the point that her husband became depressed over it. He and she are always on the seesaw. More and more tired and discouraged, Fabienne works intently at diminishing her husband, who himself continues to rise in his professional world. She devises ways to humiliate him as soon as he comes home, and she also quarrels with him about every little thing.

Her husband comes to see me and says, "I can't handle it anymore, doctor. I no longer recognize my wife. She is charming and delightful with everybody else, just as she has always been. But at home, she's becoming unendurable. Nothing pleases her, and no matter what I do, she gets after me about it. I've had all I can take, and I feel terribly tired."

I explain to him that rivalry has insinuated itself between them, the kind of jealousy that can develop between the two halves of a couple. He understands this quite well, he is open and sincere, but his wife remains impervious to these ideas and takes refuge in physical symptoms: headaches, backaches, insomnia, and so on.

Fatigue is a very bad sign in a love relationship. In my experience, few things can manage to destroy a real love; passion is able to survive all forms of jealousy regarding a third party, as we will soon discuss further. Passion can survive any sort of obstacle, but fatigue does not bode well for the relationship. It indicates that one is feeling too fed up, feeling nausea caused by the oscillations of the seesaw, the need to get off it—even if one has to do so alone. When one becomes indifferent to the game of the seesaw, from then on it no longer matters whether the other is up or down. One wants only one thing: to be neither up nor down but somewhere else where one can get some rest. Fatigue is a fatal weapon that can destroy the interdividual relation. For many couples, their rivalry is so exhausting, so enervating that they would prefer to separate.

This is what was described in a recent newspaper article: "The fashion for a 'happy divorce' has reached a high point." In 2005, it says, the number of divorces on the basis of mutual request and consent exploded. The surge tapered off a bit in 2006, but they remain a substantial majority.

What is remarkable about this is that those divorced couples then become the best friends in the world. One could say that they "rediscover each other," and after a few years some of them even get along so well that they begin to think about getting married again.

I can see only one explanation for this phenomenon. In our world, rivalry is increasing and spreading more and more widely among men and women.

A little while after they marry, many couples find themselves going up and down on the seesaw. Caught up in this hellish mutual rivalry, few succeed in changing their game. Those who do not succeed, for one reason or another, in making that change end up becoming exhausted. This leads them to renounce the game, get off the seesaw, and get divorced. They then find themselves on solid ground again and once more see each other as they used to know. Once again they find each other charming and pleasant and discover that they have a lot of interests in common.

In the case of divorced couples who think about remarrying, I advise them against it and encourage them rather to continue living separately while spending more and more weekends and vacations together, with their children if they have some. This system leaves a channel open for desire but little room for rivalry. This seems to me a wise solution, and I advocate it, even when their rivalry rises up again and rebounds against me in such comments as, "But look, this isn't a normal way of living, it's expensive, we want to be together, everybody is encouraging us to get married again," and so on.

Destroying Oneself in Order to Destroy the Other

Among some couples in the grip of that form of jealousy, when one partner begins to descend on the seesaw, he may sink lower and lower, plunging into depression or into alcohol. And if one day he begins to heal and to get better, even artificially with the help of drugs, and starts to ascend again, what does one see? That the other starts doing badly at that very moment. It could not be otherwise; there is a mechanism at work. The other starts to develop the same symptoms—alcoholism or depression, or both—in an immediate reversal of the seesaw. The second simply takes the place of the first.

Many men and women drink to get even with their partners, to try to shame them, to diminish them, or to escape from their power. It is an act of self-destruction before the omnipotence of the other, in the belief that they can force the relationship in a direction more in their own favor: drinking lets me get in a blow at the one who has been trying to dominate me, lets me impose my "disorder" on him or her, that is to say, my own order. This is, of course, an illusion.

One of my patients would regularly get drunk. When he became too drunk, his wife would have him interned in a clinic. By drinking, he was trying to weaken her and to resist her: "My wife wears me down, she's too hard on me, she bosses me around, who does she think she is?" I pointed out to him that by getting drunk he did succeed, in a certain fashion, in being disagreeable to her and not obeying her, but in the end it was he who found himself in a clinic . . . on the orders of his wife.

Because he was dominated by his wife, he started to drink. He then would have, by way of the alcohol, the feeling of hurting her and being able to drag her down. By destroying himself, he thought he could destroy her and get away with it. He imagined himself as omnipotent at the very time he was actually powerless. He spun fantasies like this precisely because he was so flattened and utterly dominated by her. I therefore explained to him that if he wanted to forcibly reverse the relation, he was using the wrong approach. He was always the more subservient of the two. If he really wanted to free himself from her authority, all he had to do was stop drinking. Then she would no longer have any means of getting him locked up. That comment made such an impression on him that he almost immediately put an end to his alcoholism. Just to understand that was enough to cure his alcoholism, although it was not enough to enable him really to escape from the rivalry. Still, it was a decisive first step.

Some couples become so devoured by rivalry that one of the two will destroy himself or herself just to destroy the other in the process. This is exactly what terrorism is: one of the two wants to blow up the world, even at the price of his or her own destruction. And in most cases the destruction is irremediable.

I once knew a couple in which the wife used to make a public display of her drinking so as to bring shame on her husband and lower him in everyone's esteem. By sinking herself deeper and deeper, she hoped to bring him down with her, dragging him along with her as she fell, doubtless because she was nursing a fierce jealousy and resentment toward him. The greater her husband's professional success, the more she began drinking at the business dinners to which they were invited, answering in his place, contradicting him and humiliating him in front of important people. He remained helpless in the face of this, unable to oppose her or to get her to keep quiet, laid low himself by a depression and despair that grew as the evening went on. Sometimes she would say to him in front of everyone, "I don't know why you're acting so attentive to that person; you told me he was an imbecile." On other occasions she would fall over dead drunk right in the middle of a dinner. Thus, little by little, she succeeded in destroying her husband, making him lose his self-confidence and the esteem of his coworkers; she finished up her work by casting doubt on his sexual potency. Eventually he lost his position and the professional success of which he had been so proud. Many men or women drive their spouses in this way to resign from their positions and renounce their ambitions.

Work as a Rival

Jealousy toward one's other half wears the mask of a third party who is used as an excuse and is accused of separating the couple: the other's work! How many women have felt jealous of their husband's work and felt themselves abandoned, neglected, and treated as of little account? More and more often now, it is the husbands who feel frustrated by the success of their wives, who may also make more money than they do. Their jealousy of their other half can make them morose and aggressive. Sometimes, if rarely, they manage to transform themselves into "house-husbands" and become content with their lot.

In the United States, one uses the expression "workaholic" to refer to men or women who devote all their time and energy to their work and their professional success. Unfortunately, the world in which we now live often forces us to sacrifice part of what should be our family time to meet the ever increasing demands of our professional milieu for performance and productivity. Many couples find themselves struggling with the impossibility of trying to keep these conflicting demands in balance.

Often one partner envies the other's success, the recognition and social prestige it brings him or her, and the way the other's career keeps smoothly advancing. The partner feels crushed by it and incapable of equaling it, of "rivalling" the other, except by trying to bring the other down by destroying his or her career. Many couples break up when one partner or the other gains a decisive promotion. If a wife is promoted to professor while her husband remains an untenured lecturer, the rivalry this sets up sometimes becomes unendurable.

If two friends work in the same company, it will be very difficult for them to keep under control the rivalry that the promotion of one or the other cannot fail to provoke. The best friends in the world cannot resist the competition that can thus insinuate itself between them. If one gains too great an advantage over the other, their friendship will quickly cease to exist, and rivalry alone will link them to one another. Each person, then, if he wants to maintain good relations and avoid exciting jealousy, must avoid speaking too openly about his successes and accomplishments, but instead attend to and appreciate the work of his collaborator or collaborators while trying not to seem superior.

Don Juanism and Messalinism

The two attitudes of frenetic and universal seduction that are known as Don Juanism and Messalinism in male and female cases respectively (after the famous Spanish seducer and the dissolute third wife of the Roman emperor Claudius) both represent a form of sexual relationship that is pure rivalry. For such predators, the other is not a partner but an object, a prey. The ephemeral "couple" they form is in reality an illusion that exists only in the mind of the prey.

A Don Juan sees women only as objects of conquest. He pursues them, lays siege to them, brings them to submission, possesses them, and then just as quickly abandons them. He casts off a woman after she has "given him all," the way an alcoholic throws away an empty bottle. Don Juans and Messalinas have only rivals everywhere. Each "object" they meet has to be taken possession of and destroyed so as to deprive a rival of it. Sometimes the rival is a real person, as when a Don Juan seduces his friends' women, or a Messalina seduces the husbands of her female friends. But more often the rivalry is so universal that every "object" that passes by must be grabbed and consumed before a rival might be able to get it.

This reminds me of the stories one hears about French peasants during the war who drank every bottle of wine they came across, saying, "One more that the Germans won't be able to drink."

Messalinas bring under submission one after another the men they collect. The first test of their power is to seduce a man and observe the way his desire becomes increasingly enslaved by their charms until he becomes totally dependent. A Messalina wants to make a man weak and abase his pride—until, behold: there is her lover, bedded, conquered, and even grateful for it. Then comes her second victory: now she is the mistress of every movement he makes. He gets dressed or gets into bed at her command and according to her whims. She plays with him a little in the manner of a bullfighter braving the bull; he exhausts his potency on the bait, while she undresses only in the last moment. Finally, she abandons him, deliberately handing him over to despair once she has completely enslaved him. He no longer interests her, and so she drops him without any sense of responsibility.

In fact, Don Juan and Messalina behave exactly like the false mother in the story of the judgment of Solomon: their only goal is to make their point of view triumph, to win a victory in their rivalry with their opposite, the legitimate possessor of the object. To win they have to dispossess the other of the object, to tear it away even at the cost of destroying it. All others are their rivals. Therefore all objects must be destroyed.

Don Juan and Messalina live in a world in which there are only preys—objects belonging to real or virtual rivals. Their rivalrous desire, therefore, will launch an attack on every object, using in the beginning the weapons of seduction and charm to bring their prey under subjection. Then they drop them, leaving them ruined and sometimes dead, no longer in a condition to belong to another—that is, to any eventual rival. Thus they make their victory complete.

Don Juan and Messalina do not understand the rivalry that moves them. Interdividual psychology reveals the mimetic mechanisms at work in their behavior. Sentiment, it is clear, plays no role in it, even if it casts at first a pink, then a red, then finally a black coloring over their relations.

Still, do they never feel anything? Are they never in love? I posed that question to one of my patients, a Messalina who was telling me she was madly in love with a man whose charms and merits she was praising to me. Naively I asked her, "Well, that one, I imagine you won't deceive him?" Her answer exploded angrily: "Oh yes I will! I don't belong to anyone. It will be a little difficult, perhaps, but I'll cheat on him in order to relativize him, to detach myself from him bit by bit, so that it will be less hard on me when I drop him!"

Another Messalina explained to me her view of men: "What is a man? A man is an accessory that I wear." When she walked down the street and came across a man who pleased her, she would always say with interest, "There's a possible affair." In reality, that woman lived in intense solitude without ever clearly realizing it. I made the comment to her that to have every man meant to have none, while to have one man was to have all of them. It was the only time I ever saw her listen to me with so much attention.

I posed the question about true love to a Don Juan who had just "conquered" one of my patients: "I hope you aren't going to deceive her, because she's sensitive and strong-minded, and if you cheat on her, she'll do the same to you, and it will be over." His answer was chilling: "Don't worry about that, Doctor; I love her, but when I'm finished with her, she'll no longer be in any condition to cheat on me or to interest herself in anyone or anything!"

These examples, among others, made me understand that sentiments are only the fleeting colorations of the mimetic relation at different stages of its evolution. It is not sentiments that determine behavior, but desire, and when desire is rivalrous, it carries everything along with it.

3. Jealousy Regarding a Third Party

Jealousy alone made me feel I was in love.

—*Madame de Lafayette*

Jealousy of a third party is the work of mimetic desire: here we have rivalries and jealousies that express themselves in threes. It often happens that there is someone who cannot be seen, a hidden mediator, who plays a decisive role in the relationship of a couple. In such cases, what one has to do is expose this person in order to defuse the conflicts he or she secretly controls. As I have already explained, rivalry is the clinical expression of mimetic desire, which is not always itself immediately visible and obvious. The work of mimetic psychotherapy must consist therefore of bringing to light this third party in order to disengage that person's surreptitious influence.

Marina comes to see me again. She is still depressed, torn between her handsome young Hubert and her older Eddy. She knows that she is suffering from not knowing what she wants and that she breaks into tears every time she tries to make a choice, that is, several times a day. She weeps when she can't decide. She weeps, therefore, all the time, and Hubert feels helpless.

"I would like to point out one detail to you," I tell Marina. "You were hesitating to separate from Eddy, but what has really plunged you into despair and brought forth all these symptoms is the fact that Eddy has linked up again with his former girlfriend, Ingrid, over whom you had previously won out. It looks to me as if it is since Eddy revealed that to you that you have broken down."

"Yes," says Marina, suddenly very attentive. "I can't stand the idea that Ingrid has taken possession of Eddy again, and you are right, it's been since that time that I've been in tears."

"Do you realize that what bothers you is not the idea of giving up Eddy but the fact that Ingrid has him back again?"

"Yes, I agree. As long as I thought Eddy was alone and was missing me, I was happy enough with Hubert, even though, as I told you before, I'm not as passionately in love with Hubert as I was—and perhaps still am—with Eddy."

"I'm going to tell you how it looks to me, and you tell me if what I say rings a bell with you. What is making you ill is not the difficulty of giving up Eddy, it's your old rivalry with Ingrid. You defeated her by taking Eddy. Now that Ingrid has Eddy back again, you see that as her victory over you, and you can't stand that."

"I understand."

I find Marina's answer very encouraging. She is honest and intelligent. She has not set herself against me, and she has not transferred her rivalry onto me so as to deny what is obvious and "shelter" her rivalry with Ingrid. Therefore, she is capable of giving it up.

"I'm going to go a step further," I say. "This triangular mechanism of which you are the victim is making you a slave to your rivalry with Ingrid and fastening you to Eddy. The more the rivalry with Ingrid eats at you, the more you feel that you love and desire Eddy."

"Yes," Marina answers, "I see. I think you've put your finger on something. I feel better already. But explain it to me further."

"The mechanism I'm talking about confers on the object of rivalry an enormous 'added value.' The way to reduce that added value is to see its mechanism clearly and relativize the rivalry. Is Ingrid really a worthy rival for you? Tell yourself two things. First, if you return to London, you will get Eddy back again, and you will be right back where you were. But in the meantime, you will probably have lost Hubert. Second, the mechanism is actually working in your favor right now in the triangle you form with Eddy and Hubert. Hubert doesn't know Eddy, he's never seen him, but he considers him a rival to be on guard against—one who is richer than he, more intelligent, and a skillful tactician. In a certain way he probably admires Eddy, since he has surely seen that his maneuver of taking Ingrid back was very adroit. But the more he admires his rival, the more in love he is with you. So in this way you are benefiting from the mechanism of rivalry instead of being its victim."

"I will think about that. I'll come back to see you again in a few days. I'm going to send Hubert to you, because he wants to meet you."

Hubert comes into my office with a big smile and a warm handshake. I feel an immediate liking for him.

"I've come to see you because I no longer feel very sure about what to do. Marina tells me you have some original ideas. Also, she's feeling better since her last visit. She's weeping less, eats a little better, and no longer bursts into tears when we make love. Why do you think that is?"

"I'd like to ask you a question: are you in love with Marina?"

"Very much. If it weren't for that, I wouldn't be here."

"Do you realize that in addition to the charm of Marina, what's stimulating your passion is the challenge you feel in getting her away from Eddy? It's your rivalry with Eddy that brings your passion to a boil and increases your desire. You want to win; you want victory." yuck.

"You're quite right. But what does Eddy have that I don't? He's old, he's sick, he can't marry her or give her children. He's immensely rich, it's true, but I'm making a very good living. What is it that makes him so attractive to Marina?"

"What attracts her is that she stands the risk of losing him, especially losing him to Ingrid. She's caught up in a game of rivalry. But you, you're at her feet, you adore her, you are with her all the time—she runs no risk of losing you. There's no game to it. Therefore, you're less exciting to her than Eddy; she feels less desire for you because regarding you her desire isn't enflamed by any rivalry."

"So my frankness, my love, all that I offer her count for nothing? In any case, I've had enough of this; I've lost a lot of the esteem I had for her, especially since I've found out that she's been telephoning Eddy behind my back. Did she tell you that? I'm sure she hasn't. She's a liar. I think I'm going to leave her; that's still the best thing for me to do."

"Don't talk nonsense," I tell him. "Psychology is 'private politics,' and one must never make a decision one won't be able to carry out."

Hubert bursts out laughing. "You're right. I can't leave her, I'm much too in love. Tell me how to get out of this jam."

"I think you ought to begin with some little changes in your own attitude. Be away more often. If she calls you in tears, tell her you are busy at the office, instead of running over and throwing yourself at her feet. And, if you can do so, tell her to take her time in thinking it over and choosing, and that while waiting you are going to go sleep over with some friends."

"Okay."

When I'm alone again, I reflect on it: I'm going to have to be on guard against identifying with Hubert, against a countertransference or even taking him for my son, since he's about the same age as mine is. But especially, I have to be careful about the triangle that might eventually take shape: Hubert, Marina, and me. I mustn't let Hubert's passion become contagious and find myself feeling similarly attracted to Marina.

Marina comes again a few days later. She clearly looks better: well made up, nicely dressed, smiling.

"I feel better," she says. "Besides, I think Eddy is not really so attached to Ingrid: he constantly telephones me and sends me emails and text messages. Of course I haven't said anything about this to Hubert, but he discovered it by poking around in my computer. He made a terrible scene about it and said he was going to leave me. He's gone to stay with some friends.

"So what did you do?"

"At first I wept alone in my bed, as usual. Then I dried my tears, and I went to the friends' place and threw myself on him."

"How did he react?"

"He was delighted! But he said again that he was going to leave me if I didn't make a clear, straightforward, and definitive choice. My parents also warned me that he'd end up getting away. I think they are right, but still, I never feel for Hubert the ardent and nervous desire that I feel for Eddy."

"Keep thinking about everything you've said, and keep trying. Play sports. We'll see each other again soon."

In my office, I go over the situation: by revealing the hidden mediator we discover what it is that makes us transfigure the object, why we give it once again a value it had lost. One then is able to relativize the feelings one brings to the object of desire and to see that they are only a coloration produced by the mimetic mechanism. The feelings don't disappear, but they find an explanation we hadn't realized. This is why the mediator must be brought to light; one can never act directly on feelings. It would be useless simply to say, "Stop being interested in that man who cannot offer you any future. Devote yourself to this new lover who is so promising." What one has to do is attack directly the source of the desire, which in this case is Marina's jealousy, and try to illuminate and devalorize the rivalry associated with the rival third party, in order to undo at its root the love she thinks still binds her to Eddy.

To devalorize the rivalry—this means, for example, to show her that the rival is not really worthy of her, that she is not a "good" mediator and doesn't merit this renewed attention. Then one might have a chance of redirecting her love onto a different path. One can act only on the patient's state of knowledge—by helping her, that is, to become conscious of the mimetic mechanism. One can exit from the mimetic mechanism only from the inside. By showing that the sentiment is an artifact, an epiphenomenon, that hides from us the mimetic mechanisms that underlie it, one can rebuild the confidence of a person who feels plunged into confusion because he or she no longer understands what is happening. Of course, one cannot reveal too abruptly the triangulations of desire that have the patient in their grip, but one can gradually enlighten her and gently help put her on the path of a real relationship.

On his side, Hubert, beneath his guise of contempt, is in the process of "divinizing" Eddy, who presents himself to him as a rival all the more to be feared because he is invisible and seems to pull Marina like a magnet. He is completely unaware of the fact that he is himself being moved by him. The rivalry he is engaged in with Eddy explains a large part of the desire he feels

for Marina. For this reason, we cannot yet be sure that he really loves her;
his interest in her is being fed by the presence of this rival third party before
whom he feels himself in a position of inferiority. In this sense, and despite
the appearances, it may be that Marina, in her vulnerability and instability,
is the one who is closest to reality and who experiences for Hubert a genuine
love (one not provoked by rivalry with a third person), and esteem and confidence in him, whereas he merely wants to snatch her away from his rival.

Hubert comes to see me, while Marina waits outside, in tears again. Gabrielle, Marina's best friend, has come to stay in their apartment in Paris for a
few days. She couldn't keep herself from immediately commenting to Marina
that she didn't look as if she was really very much in love with Hubert:
"You're not being honest with him, you ought to tell him." Marina was profoundly disconcerted. "I want to love Hubert," she said, "but I don't feel the
same passion for him that binds me to Eddy." Irritated by Marina's lying,
and doubtless in the grip of an irrepressible jealousy herself, Gabrielle went
to find Hubert and told him that Marina had just telephoned Eddy. Hubert,
deeply disturbed by this, interrogated Marina and reproached her for not
knowing what she wanted. Marina broke down again and proposed a separation. Hubert managed to keep calm, agreed to what she proposed, and began
getting his things together to leave the apartment. Marina, undone by his
apparent impassibility, threw herself at his feet and said, "You can't leave me.
If you leave me, I won't exist any longer." He felt completely dumbfounded
and no longer knew what to do, but he remained unbending and pretended
indifference.

I congratulate him for taking the appropriate approach. Eddy seemed especially attractive insofar as he could slip away to his earlier mistress, but Hubert,
by remaining unshakable and feigning detachment, became himself hard to
get. Marina is only able to desire something that is difficult or impossible to
acquire. The mechanism that inflames her desire, just as it does everywhere in
everyone, is rivalry. Hubert also took my advice and asked some of his women
friends to send him messages and phone him frequently in order to sow confusion and reignite Marina's desire by creating an impression of false rivals. It
was a matter of trying to shift toward Hubert the rivalrous mimetism that
bound Marina to Eddy through the mediation of Ingrid. Understanding the
mechanism of rivalry is not always sufficient to disengage it completely; this
is why Hubert had simultaneously to arouse a certain measure of jealousy in
order to kindle her desire and transfer the mimetic passion onto himself. These
phone calls, of course, enraged Marina, and she grilled him angrily about the
women who were after him. He adroitly reminded her that she had no grounds

to make jealous scenes, since they were no longer together. He let her imagine what she liked.

Marina comes into my office after him, still weeping. "I want only one thing," she says, "to be completely in love with Hubert, but it doesn't come, I keep on thinking about Eddy." I explain to her that the person she is really thinking endlessly about is her rival, Ingrid. I remind her that because of her hesitations, she is unfortunately about to lose Hubert. She tells me she feels completely confused. Going back to get her things in London, she saw Eddy again. She confirmed, to her great despair, that when she was with Eddy she felt peaceful and happy. I tell her that the reason she felt that way was that she had taken Ingrid's place again.

She looks at me, completely at a loss, and asks, "What can I do to fall in love with Hubert?" I explain to her that it is Ingrid alone who magnetizes her desire. For Hubert, she feels a love that is very reasonable and rational; she esteems him, he pleases her, she is in love with everything about him. I try to make her see the difference between her love for him and her love for Eddy, which is not really a difference of "love" but a difference of mimetic configuration: there is no rival third party to kindle her desire for Hubert and make him an object of rivalry. She doesn't love Hubert less, but quite the contrary, she esteems him more and in the final analysis loves him more sincerely. It is rivalry that fans the ardor of her desire for Eddy. If that rivalry managed to shift itself onto Hubert, her desire for him would take on the same intensity. I warn her, "Don't wait until he really leaves you and goes away with another woman, because then you will be madly in love with him. But it will be too late, and this time you will have genuinely objective reasons to regret it."

Passion increases only with rivalry. I help her to understand how she can little by little learn to value the love she has for Hubert. It is not a mad, passionate love, but it is a real love, one that is more authentic, imbued with tenderness and trust, and also with real generosity, a solid love on which she can build a relationship and a future. For the moment, she is not quite up to understanding this and devoting herself to that relationship, because she still reacts to the slightest movement of her rival. She remains immersed in that rivalrous reciprocity, but little by little, I hope to open her eyes sufficiently to the mechanisms that chain her to that illusory love so that she can learn to love the man she has.

Véronique is still discouraged regarding the attitude of her husband. It seems monstrous to her that he is encouraging her to take a lover so that he can use fantasies about that to revive his desire. It seems completely crazy to her. "And yet, apart from those times when he exhibits such fantasies and needs," she says, "he is adorable, a good father, a good husband, thoughtful, gentle, generous. Everyone finds him intelligent and charming. No one would imagine he was crazy."

"I don't think he's crazy. It's just that he has discovered, without realizing it, the psychological reality of mimetic desire. His desire for you may be a little weak after some years of marriage, but his feelings of love, esteem, and affection for you and your children have not changed. Unfortunately, due to who knows what circumstance, he has unexpectedly chanced upon the reality of this desire, and his mistake is that he wants to make his fantasy become reality. Could you ask him to come and see me?"

"I'll try, but I can't promise anything. If I tell him to go see a doctor, he'll tell me he's not sick. If I suggest he see a psychiatrist, he'll say he's not crazy."

"Then tell him I want to see him to talk about you, that I'm worried about your psychological equilibrium."

Albert, Véronique's husband, is a cultivated man, very artistic, elegant, somewhat timid. He comes into my office looking wary.

"You wanted to see me?"

"Yes, because I think your wife is very disturbed and that she may be on the edge of depression."

"I don't have any such feeling. What has she told you? I hope she hasn't been telling you things that are too personal."

"Yes, precisely, and that's why I wanted to see you, to tell you two things: first, that you're right: desire is stimulated by rivalry. That's a general and absolute rule, and you discovered that spontaneously. You've drawn the conclusion, correctly, on the level of psychology alone, that if your wife had a lover and told you about what she did with another man your desire would find itself revived and unleashed. On that point, you are correct. The second thing I wanted to tell you is that the game you want to get her to play is extremely dangerous. One can't manipulate psychology without consequences. Certainly, if you throw yourself from the top of the Eiffel Tower, you will experience, for a few moments, some novel and extraordinary sensations; but once you've handed yourself over to the laws of universal gravitation, you won't be able to come back to savor the experience, and you'll end up badly. In the same way, to hurl your wife into the complications of universal mimesis without a parachute, to titillate her desire that way without thinking about what might follow, could be very dangerous."

"What risk would there be? She'd experience some pleasure and would give me some. I'll desire her and love her all the more, because she would have done something extraordinary for me."

"But what about her? What would she experience? The man might become attached to her, and she to him, and if he found out that he was only being used as kindling to stimulate the desire of a third party, her husband as it happens, God only knows how he might react."

"I hadn't thought about it from that point of view."

"You are letting yourself become the plaything of your fantasies, which, I will acknowledge it again, do have a basis in reality. But for all that, human beings are not objects, and one can't play around like a sorcerer's apprentice with the laws of desire."

"I understand."

"I hope you really do understand and that you're not just saying that out of politeness. But I'm going to try to see if I can't work out some sort of compromise for you. Send your wife to me, but from now on, if you can, try to stay on the level of fantasy and don't push her in reality into the arms of another man; she just might end up staying there."

Véronique comes in looking worried. "Since he saw you, my husband seems anxious and has been looking at me distrustfully. He's become jealous and now suspects me of wanting to leave him. I don't understand what's going on."

"You husband is suffering. You love him. Let's try to find a compromise, even if it might seem a little 'twisted': on the one hand, reassure him by telling him that you love only him; on the other hand, tell him about the effect some movie star has on you and let your imagination run, describe the feelings you would experience if he kissed you the way he kisses his partner in the film, and what would happen after that. That might help your husband, and at least there wouldn't be any danger of the actor coming out of the screen and jumping on you."

A few years later I see Véronique again. "My husband has calmed down," she says. "He never talks to me about that sort of thing any more. I tried to do what you said, but clearly movies don't interest him. We no longer make love at all, but we're living happily, and there are many things we share. The children are growing up. As for me, I've resigned myself to the situation."

Virginia, tired of the lover who keeps going away with his luggage and coming back, looks at me with a bewildered air and asks, "What's a yo-yo husband?"

"It's a man who hasn't understood that desire requires a choice and also that abandoning someone forever feels the same as a prohibition. The prohibition then rekindles the desire for what was abandoned."

"I don't understand."

"It is a man who cannot sustain his desire for a woman, keep it going for a long period, who can't make a definite choice, but who, after a while, finds his desire revived for the woman who was abandoned and "lost." This reversal on his part clothes itself with noble sentiments: the call of duty, pity, the needs of the family, the children, and so on."

"So, he doesn't really love me?"

"No, I am sure he does love you, but that is not enough to keep him with you."

"When he goes back to his wife, he keeps calling me to tell me he misses me, that he loves me, that he can't live without me; then one fine day, he's back and it starts all over again. I'm exhausted. What should I do?"

"I cannot tell you what you need to do, nor what you ought to do. This sort of man is never able to come to a definite decision."

"What it adds up to, then, is that he wants both of us!"

"Yes. And if you make some compromises and accept his repeated disappearances, this could go on for a long time."

"No, I love him, certainly, but I am still able to make a life for myself. I'm not going to wear out my patience waiting for him to come back and then waiting again for him to leave. I'm going to leave him and escape from all that."

Gérard comes into my office, looking sad and lost. He's a man about fifty years old, an architect with a brilliant, successful career. He tells me his story: "I'm in a terrible state. I have been living for three years now with a thirty-year-old woman. During the last six months, she's become frigid and mean. She's cheated on me with several men. I know it, because I followed her. I've spent nights tracking her through Paris; I've even bought electronic gadgets to listen to her phone calls or to be able to follow her car. I've lost twenty-two pounds in six months. Ten days ago, she disappeared and asked me not to try to see her again. Since then I no longer feel as if I exist at all. I don't do anything, I don't understand anything, and I feel urges toward suicide that worry my friends so much that they've made me come to see you."

"Yes, you certainly are depressed, but antidepressants wouldn't help you, because classic depression is an illness of mood. But you are in a much more complicated predicament: you no longer exist!"

"That's exactly what it is! Moreover, I feel as if I never have existed; I feel as if I'm nothing!"

"Because she has abandoned you, you think you're nothing. She's left you as if there was nothing there. She has not simply left you, by the way, she has nullified you; it is as though she pressed the *delete* key of her computer."

"But why? I gave her money, clothes, jewelry, all the love in the world. During our last conversation, she said I brought nothing to her. I found the strength to tell her that the love of a man like me is not nothing. She smiled, and my heart leaped. But she left anyway."

"I am going to try to explain something to you: we are changing structures, perpetually in a state of becoming. It is desire that engenders the self and causes it to exist. Desire presides over all human relationships, and I do not need to tell you how strong the desire was that united you with your girlfriend. Nor how it has been whipped up into a devouring passion during the last few months while you were finding rivals on every street corner. The desire that united you with your girlfriend constituted, created in you, a *self*, a self-of-desire, a self-of-that-particular-desire. The abrupt departure of your girlfriend destroyed that self, which had become the whole of you. The sudden break resulted in that desire suddenly ceasing to animate that self. You look into yourself and find yourself gripped by a veritable death anguish, which is a terrible suffering that drives you to think about suicide as the only possible solution for putting an end to the suffering."

"Then there is nothing I can do?"

"To begin with, try to reconnect with all of your past selves: the ones you shared with your wife, with your children, with your friends. Remember that you had a life before her. Invest yourself in your work. There is a professional self that you have to recover and give preeminence to during this period. Then one day, perhaps, you will meet another woman and another desire will again build up another self for you.

"I don't know if I will succeed in that. I'm not sure either that I've understood all you've been saying. I do realize, though, that I owe myself to my wife, who is not to be discounted, to my children, to my friends, and to my business."

Gérard suffered for two years, but he didn't commit suicide.

Can One Rescue a Relationship?

Love, too, has to be learned.

—*Nietzsche*

The first comment I would like to make to conclude all these reflections is that diagnosis must precede treatment. Diagnosis in the kind of cases we have been talking about must first of all include assuring ourselves that the members of the couple are of good will, that is, that they wish to get out of their predicament, that they are willing to consider new ideas, and that they have decided to view the therapist as an ally rather than as an adversary or rival whose worthlessness, at best, or whose toxicity, at worst, has to be demonstrated. At least one of the two partners must meet these criteria if a therapeutic effort is to have any chance of succeeding.

We have seen above in numerous examples that in order to overcome jealousy regarding a third party, the rival has to be brought to light and demystified.

In other cultures, a husband might guard against any possible rival third party by hiding his wife under veils of varying degrees of thickness, right up to the point of total covering by a burka. As an Egyptian proverb puts it, "If the eye doesn't see, the heart doesn't suffer." In Mediterranean cultures, one is careful to avoid the evil eye; an eye that looks on what I have is "evil," because its gaze can result in mimesis of appropriation and consequently rivalry. Therefore one must hide every object whose sight might give rise to another's desire and arouse rivalry—especially one's wife (or wives)!

Mitigating one partner's jealousy regarding the other partner's qualities and accomplishments is much more difficult, as we have seen. Once rivalry has taken root in the relationship of a couple, it is very hard to uproot. I gave several examples above.

Here, I believe, preventive measures are much more effective than curative ones. We should teach young people, even before they fall in love and form a couple, about the way mimetic desire works and about the innumerable snares of rivalry and the dangerous reality of universal mimesis.

Unfortunately, young couples charge head first into the adventure of love without having patience to prepare themselves for it. Still, some sincere and well-meaning ones do learn, little by little during the course of their life together, to see and understand the reality of desire. To do this is not a purely intellectual procedure; it is a matter of initiation, in the sense that it involves a gradual transformation of the person involved, as he or she advances in it.

The ultimate goal of this sort of initiatory development is to liberate desire from the rivalry that is intimately intermixed with it. The result, when it is successful, is a gradual acquisition of wisdom, that is, of the capacity to desire what one has.

Generally speaking, how can one protect a relationship from the rivalry that threatens it? As I have said, and as we have seen in the cases described above, love is highly vulnerable. This is true not only because love is in constant need of care and attention in order to grow, but also, and especially, because it must be protected in every moment from the rivalry that can insinuate itself within it and put it in danger of being perverted and even destroyed.

The path is arduous, but it is far from impossible. Often just to bring the mimetic mechanisms to light is enough to defuse them. If one member of the couple is sufficiently alert and is warned about the problems of rivalry, he or she can to some degree counteract them, and even protect the other from his or her slips with regard to them. But this watchfulness must be constant and carried out with full consciousness. It is a form of ascesis, and it calls for a real conversion. It is this that is perhaps the greatest difficulty. I often tell my patients, in order to awaken their attention, "When you go home, you will be like a trainer entering the cage of a tiger." The whip is only useful if it is never used. This image allegorically represents two things that are essential:

constant watchfulness to avoid any movement, any gesture, any word capable of setting rivalry, aggression, or resentment in motion—and the absence of fear. Many, indeed, are the spouses who are afraid of their husbands or their wives. Such fear is debilitating and a poor guide for dealing with problems. It can ruin relationships. One might even say that the fear of rivalry is worse, for the health of a couple, than is open conflict.

Whatever may be the depth of one's feelings, they are not alone enough to nurture a relationship, protect it, and make it live. One must never lose sight of the fact that love can be blown up at any moment by stepping on a mimetic mine. If you were driving a truck loaded with TNT, ready to explode at the least jolt, you wouldn't have to be any more careful! Avoiding even the smallest stone that could cause disaster, keeping one's eyes always open. Saadi, a great Sufi master in the thirteenth century, gave us a precious piece of advice: "Friendships that have taken a whole lifetime to ripen should not be broken in an instant. Be careful, when you hold a stone, not to break a ruby that has taken years to be formed."[1]

Any friendship, any love, no matter how great it might be, can in fact be broken by a small and apparently harmless jealousy that can suddenly take root and undo its fragile equilibrium, making one lose one's trust in the other. An unfortunate word, an allusion to some third party, an imaginary suspicion, a clumsy reproach, and the serpent of jealousy or rivalry is quick to slither in and make us lose sight of the love that connects us.

In L'Amour fou ("Mad Love"), André Breton sums up in a few words what such a broken relationship is like: "The attraction is broken; even the loveliness of the beloved face goes into hiding; a wind of ashes sweeps everything away; the pursuit of life is compromised."[2]

When rivalry slips into and begins to invade a relationship, it can undo that relationship just as surely as love had built it up.

Another difficulty doubtless derives from the fact that many men and women attribute to love a capricious, ephemeral, and volatile character. They also tend to believe that love can withdraw as easily as it came, in an instant; that its lifetime is inherently limited so that there is no point in trying to preserve it; and that to try to do so would only increase love's eventual disappointment and exhaustion and hasten the disenchantment to which, by its very nature, it is condemned. Nevertheless, love should be continuously constructed and strengthened. Its maturation requires time and intelligence—it is never fortified in advance against our weaknesses and the reefs onto which our desire can wash us. "In the closest kiss, the dearest touch, there is the small gulf which is none the less complete because it is so narrow, so nearly non-existent," wrote D. H. Lawrence.[3] Unfortunately, love does not protect us at all from envy, covetousness, jealousy, or the need to control and dominate the other. That is not, however, a sign of love's weakness or its illusoriness but only of the constantly renewed attention that should be given to it.

One must therefore understand that all through their life together, a couple will have to "manage" a power relationship, a relationship of latent rivalry, no matter how the couple's relationship might have been built up, no matter how deep and strong may be its ties, no matter how happily the spouses may be united.

The Politics of Love

The couples who come to see me have usually been involved for a long time, sometimes even for years, in relationships that are conflictual and painful, wrestling with jealousies about a third party (an external rival) or about the other half (the members having become rivals of one another), unable to find the peace and fulfillment they once experienced together, and without any idea how they ended up in that situation. To many, the only way out they can imagine seems to lie in separation, and yet, still hoping for some solution, they cannot or will not decide on that. Some never see how attached they are to their rivalry, and they cannot imagine sacrificing that for the sake of a peaceful love. Rivalry can sometimes be a much more powerful glue than the love that preceded it.

I would like to offer some simple counsels, some *strategies* for loving, what one might call "a psychological politics of love," which the members of every couple should keep in mind from the moment they set forth on the difficult path of a shared life. Most of these strategies require nothing more than a clear understanding of the mimetic mechanisms and of the logic of rivalry that they induce.

Even if we can never escape from the mimesis that runs through us and manipulates us, one may, on the other hand, orient it and illuminate it so as to reestablish real dialogue in a couple's relationship. One must first work on refreshing language, cleansing it of anything that might risk creating or maintaining the game of rivalry. And by means of that language, one must work to preserve an appropriate distance, the distance needed for real exchange—that is, neither too far nor too close. The ways and the language the members of a couple find to speak to one another can have the effect of intensifying or eliminating rivalry. Diplomats have long been trained in this sort of practice, and a loving relationship requires a similar adroitness and delicacy in the choice of words.

Perhaps this is what a certain Jewish joke, in its own special manner, indirectly reveals:

> One man congratulates another: "Good for you! After twenty-five years you're still speaking tender little words to your wife: my darling, my sweet-heart, my treasure, and so on! You must certainly have a secret!"
>
> "No, you won't believe me, but I've simply forgotten her name!"

No longer to know the public name of someone one loves . . . To find a new name for her, to give her a name that is only for the two of us. We know how creative is the act of naming, how it takes ownership, how it gives life to a relationship in which we become reborn. Quite often, indeed, a relationship takes solid shape when each partner gives a special name to the one he or she loves, as though in a new baptism. By that very act the partners indicate that their relationship is unique and essential. In a crisis, on the other hand, in moments of anger, one can also observe how they may suddenly return to using their ordinary given names.

Still another important truth is expressed in such changing of names and forgetting of the partner's ordinary forename. The key to love resides also in recognizing the mystery of the other, in understanding that I could never pos-sess, circumscribe, and define the one I love, nor enclose her within a defini-tively named identity. To understand that she will always escape my grasp and that it is that very liberty I must try to preserve, without seeking to constrain it, because that is what enables us to maintain our love, which nourishes itself on mystery and on our joint, repeated recognition of its mysteriousness.

Warning Signs of Rivalry

It is at the beginning of conflict, when the first symptoms of mimetic rivalry appear, that it is easiest to counteract them and save the relationship. But one must be quick to recognize and understand these symptoms so that one can move to interrupt them. The warning signs of a crisis can be quite varied: reproaches, contempt, depreciation, or even indifference. And once they have taken hold, they all evoke increasing rivalry. Someone who feels devalued or rejected will in his or her turn be tempted to respond with reproaches and rejection. Reciprocity feeds rivalry more and more, in a vicious circle than can take deep root in a couple's relationship and finally make it explode.

The endless reproaches can take innumerable forms: "It is your fault if . . . ," "You ought to have . . . ," "You should . . . ," "You have never . . . ," "You always . . . ," "You shouldn't. . . ." Certainly, no couple is ever completely free from ordinary little reproaches, but if some are acceptable and only occasional, others can quickly become unbearable and invasive and be repeated to the point that they nourish increasing rivalry. If my wife tells me, "You shouldn't drink at midday," I can hear that and understand her concern. On the other hand, if she goes on to say, "You shouldn't eat that, it'll make you fat," or "You shouldn't put on so much salt," these injunctions will soon begin to irritate me and make me feel a need to retaliate in order to protect my space and my freedom. I will resent these sorts of remarks as so many ways of trying to control me, limit me, infantilize me. Such control is a seizing of power, a way of affirming one's authority and superiority over another. It is also a reification of the person and the relationship. To prevent one's spouse from doing something, such as speaking, for example, or to speak in her place, is to lose the proper distance from her, to begin to confuse one's roles. To put words in another's mouth is also to close off the possibility of dialogue; it is to do the questioning and the answering all by oneself.

A woman who wishes to turn resolutely toward a new future with her husband must learn to begin talking with him differently, refusing to engage in any dialogue that begins with "I" or "you," and speaking only in terms of "we" or "us." By doing so, one names the relationship and one can bring it to life again. Such a woman should say to her husband, "We have a problem, and we're going to try to deal with it together. Let's do everything we can to be happy from now on." She should set aside all accusations—such as, "You haven't . . . ," "You ought to . . . ," "You did . . ."—and talk with him about the problems of the relationship, which from now on will be "ours." The use of "we" gives us a way of placing ourselves back into real relationship when the relationship has degenerated into rivalry.

Many insidious reproaches begin with statements like "If I were in your place. . . ." This is a way of setting up a comparison, and comparisons can quickly stir up and favor rivalry and then conflict. If a woman says to her husband, "You shouldn't let your boss speak to you like that, you ought to have the courage to tell him what you think . . . ," she implies that if she were in his place, she wouldn't let it happen, that she wouldn't humble herself before a boss. Thus she sets up a comparison and therefore a rivalry, an immediate power struggle. She basically gives him to understand that he does not amount to much and that she is a lot stronger than he is. Talking in such a manner can also be a way of setting the bar very high, suggesting to her husband that he doesn't live up to the appropriate standard. Even what might look like a high valuation of her husband in comparison with others often masks an extreme demand on him: "You can't let yourself be treated that way by incompetents," "You're too good for . . . ," "If I had your talent, I'd. . . ." It lets one insidiously diminish one's spouse while exalting oneself.

Indifference or silence can also be a frequent form of aggression. If a woman is faced with silence on the part of her husband, then no matter what she says, she will feel herself despised, rejected, treated as of little worth. She will feel as if she counts for nothing and will begin to lower her estimation of herself, which will in turn lead her to hold this against her husband fiercely. Because she no longer has the feeling that she exists in his sight, she will try in every way she can to provoke him, to get some reaction from him, to shake him out of his indifference, and will end up eliciting aggressiveness and hostility from him in turn. The only consequence of this will be to redouble his contempt and his apathy with regard to her. And on her side, it will only increase her own ill temper and anger.

Rivalry always comes from too much proximity; beyond a certain degree of closeness, rivalrous fusion will put an end to dialogue. Words will no longer be able to circulate freely between the two members of the couple; the coalescence of the spouses will become complete, as at the peak of a battle. Neither actually says anything anymore; each approaches the adversary only the better to get in a blow and bring him or her to submission. The intensity of rivalry becomes so great among some couples that they can no longer speak to one another. Every word is immediately interpreted as an act of aggression or of counteraggression. Silence, too, can quickly become a terrible weapon used to signify to the other one's own superiority. What exacerbates the conflict, the excessive closeness that rivalry involves, is also what separates the protagonists. They lose sight of each other precisely because they are too close to one another. To restore dialogue, in order to be able to reunite the couple and "open" it up in a helpful way, will require reestablishing and maintaining some distance. Where there is no distance, there can be no dialogue, and without dialogue, there can be no relationship. But for this to happen, each must be willing to renounce a relationship of force.

Turning Together toward the Future

Couples can succeed in maintaining their relationship only if they preserve a constant vigilance to prevent these sorts of slip ups. Let us consider Adam and Eve once again. Adam would have to be careful to avoid reproaching Eve for causing the problem: "If you hadn't talked with the serpent, if you hadn't said . . . , if you'd listened to me. . . ." Every time one opens a door to reproaches, rivalry rushes in, and the couple's relationship is threatened. To prevent this happening, each partner must voluntarily and consciously make a constantly renewed effort to protect the relationship, lest it slip away into a facile rivalry. I have confirmed this many times over: whenever a dispute begins or a problem arises, old stories and old griefs come to the surface again. A husband told me how his wife, from time to time, in the middle of a conversation about something, even something rather pleasant, would suddenly begin going over old mistakes of his and berating him again: "You know you didn't take me to Venice in 1999, even though you promised you would." I have dubbed this sort of impromptu reappearance of a long-ago event at the moment we least expect it "the computer-gone-haywire syndrome." There is nothing like it for bringing a conflict back to life.

Adam, if he wants to get hold of the situation and permanently calm the tensions at the heart of his marriage, must avoid everything that has provoked rivalry in the past and that risks reawakening it: references to a third party, real or symbolic, comparisons between the two of them. He must not keep on reproaching Eve for talking with the serpent or eating the apple. It also requires knowing how to put paid to old accounts, knowing how to forgive and turn toward the future together. If Adam wants to stay with Eve, to give her children, and to have a harmonious life together, he must not keep talking about yesterday's mistakes but rather talk with her about how they are going to build their house, about projects they can undertake and share in. He has to understand that his interest is in the present flourishing of their relationship, and has to stop replaying old lost battles with her. It is in this way that transcendence can reappear, the peaceful third element that is indispensable to every successful relationship.

Occasions When a Rival Third Can Reunite a Couple: A Good Use for Mimesis

Now and then, when desire seems to have grown too weak in a couple, I suggest that one of them create an imaginary rival third party to liven it up and reawaken the interest and love of the other by arousing jealousy over the unexpected emergence of an obstacle. Once a close friend of mine, coming to confide in me, was in despair over seeing her marital relationship become strained. "I can't go on," she said. "My husband is deceiving me and leaves me on my own." This very beautiful woman in her fifties was experiencing an exhausted relation with him. They had two children, and there did not seem to be anything in particular coming between them. Nevertheless, she discovered that her husband had for several months been having an affair with a very young woman. She told me that her husband's disinterest in her saddened her much more than did this liaison and that she would do anything to win him back. How could she do it? This was an intelligent woman; I urged her to create an imaginary personage, whom we would call Marcus, and to talk about him to her friends, especially to those she knew would pass on indiscreet confidences to her husband.

She managed in this way to bring this imaginary individual to life so skillfully and so effectively that her husband ended up hearing about the existence of this man and developing real suspicions about him. One day, he came to ask me about this mysterious person his wife was keeping company with. I assured him that I knew nothing. He became quite disturbed, telling me she was seeing him regularly. I then suggested to him that perhaps it wasn't too late to win her back. A few weeks later he finally made up his mind to leave his young mistress in order to devote himself to reawakening the desire of his wife, which he thought had died out. Here was a case of mimetic manipulation, but one in which one knew what one was doing. The result was a happy one.

Becoming Willing to Renounce Rivalry

How can rivalry within a couple be avoided? Isn't there always one partner who tends to be dominant? Isn't there always some degree of inequality built into the relationship? If the couple is to hold together, it is especially necessary that the partners not let themselves get involved in games of rivalry. But the ideal of equality can tend itself to become a source of rivalry as soon as some little bit of inequality creeps into the relationship. I think, therefore, that it is necessary for a couple to accept some measure of mutually agreed-on inequality, a balance, a difference that both acknowledge, a form of selective hierarchy. One or the other must be allowed to take the lead.

When a couple is on a seesaw, it is lost. If one obtains a position in Lille and the other a position in Marseille, and neither is willing to renounce success in his or her career, a struggle for power will spring up immediately and the relationship will find itself at an impasse. One of the two will have to renounce the object of his or her desire for the sake of the other's desire. Rivalry has to be sacrificed in order to allow love to live. And in this sense, the one who truly loves is doubtless the one who renounces the object of his or her desire in order to preserve the relationship.

But once rivalry has taken root, how can one disarm it and establish a new harmonious relationship? This will require an extraordinary agility on the part of the partner who is in the higher, dominant position. The leading partner must make the other think that he (or she) is more vulnerable than he really is, by showing little weaknesses in areas that are not very important. He might say, for example, "I'm ill," "I feel depressed," "I've lost money," "I feel sad," "I'm tired," and so on. It can be helpful to be a little negative about oneself, while always affirming, listening to, and looking to one's spouse, taking the time to give him or her importance, attention, and support, before talking about oneself, one's accomplishments and successes—things that could risk provoking and diminishing the other unintentionally.

This also demands that one avoid responding to what might seem indications of rivalry, in order to do away with any seeds of potential discord before they can sprout. One must also help the other to understand that to renounce rivalry can actually strengthen one's own self-esteem—that it is not a matter of submission but of superiority, perhaps even of a superiority so great that it may be invisible to the other. I can be superior to the other, without his or her realizing it, if I humble myself in full consciousness that I am doing so to avoid rivalry.

Children: The Incarnation of the Relationship

The arrival of a child is a real upheaval in the life of a couple. An equilibrium patiently developed is often abruptly broken and must be completely rethought and achieved all over again. In many cases, the child becomes a new rival. The father may suddenly become jealous, feeling excluded from the close bond between the mother and her baby. He may find it hard to accept that the mother no longer gives him the same attention and is no longer as available as she was. He may feel resentful toward the child for depriving him of the exclusive love that he previously enjoyed. Even if he cannot always formulate these feelings clearly, and in a way that does not make him feel guilty about feeling them, he may feel himself to be in competition with the child who is now depriving him of his wife's full presence. Indeed the mother really is much less available: "baby blues," lactation, hormonal changes, fatigue, and disturbed sleep wear her down and affect her mood. The irritability she shows can sometimes be experienced painfully by her husband, who cannot always talk about his own frustration and the feelings of rejection that assail him; because, in his eyes, the infant is untouchable, and he cannot speak critically about it without seeming unnatural. One of the oldest solutions, and the most effective, is to introduce another third party—an aunt, a grandmother, a sister, a cousin, or a nursemaid—who will take charge of the child occasionally so as to let the couple get some sleep, rediscover each other, and refresh their marital bond.

Some parents, in the grip of the difficulties they may be having as a couple, in the form of rivalry or jealousy, also make use of the child as a means of more effectively separating themselves, or else of reconciling with each other for the child's sake.

A child can also become a weapon of aggression for a couple that is splitting apart. A wife who wants to dominate her husband may reproach him for not being around enough, or may ask him to give the child its bath, or contradict him in front of the child, or disturb the child frequently so that her husband will have to take care of it. The child thus gets used against the other partner in order to constrain or dominate him or her. This is particularly prominent in the case of divorces: each wants to gain an advantage while appearing to be serving the interests of the child, and so they give themselves over, in the name of the noblest reasons, to open warfare, which can escalate to a rare degree of violence. The child becomes literally sacrificed to the rivalry of the parents, who nevertheless both claim they are acting only for the welfare of the child. Many messy divorces are in reality symbolic sacrifices. The child can come out of it injured and severely stressed. Completely reified in the thick of the rivalry, turned into an object to fight over, the child is allowed no space in which to exist for its own sake. The alternative, nevertheless, is quite simple. It is what I formulated earlier in interpreting the story of the judgment of Solomon: either one chooses to sacrifice the child to the rivalry or one sacrifices the rivalry for the sake of the child. A moment comes when both partners must acknowledge the need to abandon their rivalry and ally themselves with one another, whatever differences they may have, in order to find together the necessary means for the real good of the child, who must be protected and respected.

The child is, in a sense, the vector of the relationship between its parents: it can be the emanation of the couple's harmony, the incarnation of its alliance, or the object of its rivalry. If the child becomes an object the partners try to tear away from each other, this is a sign that the relationship has become blocked. The reification of the child, the reduction of the child to a bone of contention, is a symptom that shows that the relationship of the parents has become rivalrous.

It also frequently happens that a couple will break up after the birth of a second, or third, or even a fourth child. Every new birth turns out each time to be the occasion for a new effort of regulation of the conflicts that separate the parents. The child becomes a token of the relationship, a currency of exchange. In this sense, the child is sacrificed in the very moment it is conceived.

I once knew a young couple who had already had two children. The young woman went through periods of depression related to her own past, and her husband began having affairs. Then he got the idea of having a third child, in order to reassure his wife, to prove his good will to her and try to repair their relationship, which had been weakened by his repeated liaisons. The child thus took on the character of a gift, of a proof of love and faithfulness. The wife herself accepted the child as a pledge of her forgiveness. The child therefore came into the world to hold their marriage together, and yet a year later they divorced. The child was obviously unable to repair the relationship, to reconcile and reunite its parents, who had not themselves actually done anything to resolve their differences. But the child will long bear the burden of guilt for their separation.

In this case, the child was not considered for what it was in itself. The event of its birth was not thought about in the way it should have been. Its birth was not experienced as an event in its own right but as a sort of glue that had been brought in to cement the breaks in the relationship. The child was instrumentalized and thereby symbolically sacrificed.

A child incarnates the relationship of its parents. That is why, in the same way as love itself, the child must be protected. If a couple, overburdened by their work, forget their child and do not give it sufficient attention, it puts not only the child in jeopardy but the marriage as well. The happy and harmonious development of a child is a reflection of the relation of its parents both with each other and with the child.

Once a young boy was brought to me who had set fire to his house. He was a very intelligent child, exactly six years old. I asked him, "Why did you light the fire? Your parents are very upset." He answered, "What about them? What do you think *they* do?" He thus indicated to me that in setting fire to the house, he was only imitating them, revealing the symbolic conflagration that had already broken out between his parents and that was threatening their life as a family.

To Give Time to Love

In a peaceful love relationship, not only must there be an appropriate amount of distance, so as to reduce the possibility of rivalry, but that distance must also, and above all, be inscribed in the dimension of time as openness to the future. Love is never given all at once and completely, in the form of an immediate closeness; it is never reducible to the mere mutual presence of the lovers. It seems to me that love is always ahead of itself, one might say, somewhere up ahead of the couple who are learning to knit it into their lives, to make it real anew in each moment. And because love is always in motion, it always has to be reborn—given and received in the same moment that it escapes from us.

Love's "story" should be thought of not as running along a straight line, already defined and imaginatively present, but as a door opening onto a multiplicity of paths that can be taken. In order to flourish, a relationship needs a specific time, which can give it a sense of always being open, multiple, and new. Love invents itself, creates itself every day. This is where the greatest difficulty can be experienced in trying to leave behind rivalrous mimetism and neurotic repetition, since they make us replay the same stories over and over, binding us in a closed cycle of time. When time becomes simply repetitive and no longer creative, this indicates that we are stuck in the past, in the snare of loves already played out, in an endless settling of old accounts—enslavement to the same old models. One must learn to make love live, so that it can be free, always fluid in its manifestations and forms. Because love cannot remain statically identical with itself without dying away, any more than we ourselves can.

* * *

How can one give new birth to a love that seems dead? There is no recipe.

Because it is *both* of yesterday's lovers *together* who are locked in the mimetic hell, it is *both together* who will be able, if they want to, to leave it. But one must understand clearly, once again, that despite all psychotherapeutic efforts, one cannot command feelings. To say, "Love one another" may be an admirable formula on the level of morality; but on the level of psychology, it would presuppose that the problem had already been solved.

In reality, the task of mimetic psychotherapy will be to diminish rivalry, and once its mechanism has been brought to light and "unplugged," the sentiments with which it clothes itself (hatred, jealousy, antipathy, and so on) will disappear. The mechanism of mimesis, free then to evolve toward nonrivalrous relations, will instead clothe itself quite naturally in affectionate feelings.

Notes

Introduction

1. "Mirror Neurons and Imitation Learning as the Driving Force behind 'the Great Leap Forward' in Human Evolution," *Edge* 69 (June 1, 2000).

2. René Girard, *Deceit, Desire, and the Novel: Self and Other in Literary Structure*, trans. Yvonne Freccero (Baltimore: Johns Hopkins University Press, 1965). The original title in French was *Mensonge romantique et vérité romanesque*, literally "romantic lying and novelistic truth."

3. René Girard, Jean-Michel Oughourlian, and Guy Lefort, *Things Hidden since the Foundation of the World*, trans. Stephen Bann and Michael Metteer (Stanford, CA: Stanford University Press, 1987).

4. Jean-Michel Oughourlian, *The Puppet of Desire: The Psychology of Hysteria, Possession, and Hypnosis*, trans. Eugene Webb (Stanford, CA: Stanford University Press, 1991).

Chapter One. Psychological Movement

1. Pierre Corneille, *Le Cid*, act I, scene 6.

2. [A series of letters published in French in 1669, claiming to be a translation by Gabriel Joseph de Lavergne, the Vicomte de Guilleragues, of letters by Mariana Alcoforado, a Portuguese nun, to her lover, a French officer, the Comte de Saint-Léger, a real historical figure. Their authenticity has been controversial, but they have had great literary influence. —Trans.]

3. "Ordure, mon amour." [This was a change of plot in the 1955 film (not present in the 1926 version filmed by Jean Renoir, which followed Zola more closely), but the film version illustrates Oughourlian's idea nicely. In the actual novel by Emile Zola, Muffat withdraws quietly after being cast off by Nana; then sometime later, Nana dies of smallpox. —Trans.]

4. Georges Bataille, *L'Alleluiah* (Paris: Gallimard, coll. "L'Imaginaire," 1998).

5. [The author here is referring to Milton H. Erickson (1901–1980), a leading figure in the field of hypnotherapy. —Trans.]

6. The term "subject" should be understood here in its broadest sense, not as an independent entity, but as an open ensemble in constant interaction with the other "subjects" that surround it.

7. [Pierre Janet (1859–1947) was especially known for his studies of hysteria, which he sometimes experimented with hypnosis to investigate. —Trans.]

CHAPTER TWO. THE CREATION AND THE FALL

1. Genesis, *New Jerusalem Bible* (New York: Doubleday, 1999), the English translation of the French *La Bible de Jérusalem* (Paris: Cerf, 1961). All Biblical quotations will be from this version unless otherwise specified.

2. *Oeuvres de Gabriel Tarde,* vol. 1, *Monadologie et Sociologie,* Collection "Les Empecheurs de penser en rond," Institut Synthélabo pour le progrès de la connaissance, Le Plessis-Robinson, 1999, p. 73.

3. Paul Ricoeur, *The Symbolism of Evil,* trans. Emerson Buchanan (Boston: Beacon Press, 1969), 251.

4. Ibid., 236.

5. Josy Eisenberg and Armand Abécassis, *A Bible ouverte. II, Et Dieu créa Éve.* "Présences du judaïsme" (Paris: Albin Michel, 1979), 50. This title will be referred to subsequently as *Bible ouverte.*

6. Aristotle, *Poetics,* 4:2 (1448b5), trans. Ingram Bywater, in *The Basic Works of Aristotle,* ed. Richard McKeon (New York: Random House, 1941), 1457.

7. [In these two sentences, the author uses two different French words, both of which are usually translated as "knowledge." The "*connaissance*" of good and evil, in the first sentence, connotes understanding or intimate acquaintance; "*savoir,*" in the second sentence, has the other connotations that I have taken the liberty of spelling out in the translation. —Trans.]

8. Eisenberg and Abécassis, *Bible ouverte,* 70.

9. Ibid., 71.

10. André Chouraqui, *La Bible* (Paris: Desclee de Brouwer, 1989). [The French word in this quotation that I have translated as "the one of earth" is "*le glébeux,*" an adjective made from *le glèbe* (earth, soil, clod), which is clearly intended by Chouraqui as a literal translation of the name of Adam in Hebrew, which means "earth." The French *contre* is commonly

translated as "against" but can be also translated as "next to," "contrary to," "counter to," and so on. I have chosen "opposite" as most appropriate for conveying the suggestions of both "contrary to" and "next to." —Trans.]

11. [A popular French playwright well known for his misogynistic humor. —Trans.]

12. Eisenberg and Abécassis, *Bible ouverte,* 139.

13. I should note that Chouraqui's translation of this word as "naked" will probably seem problematic to scholars of Hebrew. The Semitic root of the word in Hebrew is '-r-m (i.e., *'ayin-resh-mem*) meaning "crafty, shrewd" (as in the Bible de Jérusalem's translation, "le plus *rusé*"). The root for the Hebrew word for "naked," on the other hand, is '-w-r (i.e., *'ayin-waw-resh*). If Gen 3:1 were using the root of that word, the vocalization would be *'arom,* but actually it is *'arum.* The two words are, therefore, etymologically distinct. The similarity of the two words and their proximity in the Biblical text does suggest, however, that the choice of this word in Gen. 3:1 was intended by the Biblical author or authors as a play on Gen 3:10–11, where the Hebrew word for "naked" *does* appear ("Who told you that you were naked?"). Chouraqui's translation brings that interpretive possibility to attention, and if the text can be interpreted as involving such a play on the two words, that would also suggest the important psychological insight I will be using Chouraqui's translation to develop.

14. Ricoeur, *Symbolism of Evil,* 256. Ricoeur also notes in this connection: " … it is already clear that the dialectic of lust overflows the adventure of the *libido* on every side. … the symbolism of the serpent opens up and uncovers an immense field for 'lust,' of which sexuality is only one sector" (256, note 12).

15. Ibid.

16. Deuteronomy 5:21 (in Chouraqui's translation, with my own italics): "You shall not *covet* the wife of your companion, you shall not desire your neighbor's house, his field, his servant, his cow, his ass, *nor all that belongs to your companion.*" Appropriative mimesis is here identified as *the* danger *par excellence.* The text of Deuteronomy makes explicit what God prescribes. In Genesis, God simply states the permanent danger constituted by mimetic desire (the lineage of the serpent) for human beings (the lineage of the woman). The tenth commandment puts the dots on the "i"s.

17. Tarantulism is a strange illness found in Apulia in southern Italy. It is supposed to be due to a bite from a tarantula. The person affected by it begins to imitate the spider, to identify with it, and to dance as if possessed by the creature. This imitation can go on for several days. Like the serpent, the spider images otherness: by its bite it injects its venom into the victim, transmits to him its desire. We can see there the working of the mimetic mechanism in its pure form: possessed by the desire of the other, the person "tarantulaed" begins first to identify himself with his model, miming the dance of the spider. Next, he enacts the mimetic relation itself, miming his rivalrous relation to the model: he dances as though he is trying to crush the spider.

18. *Je t'aime—tout sur la passion amoureuse* (Paris: Plon, 1997). English-language edition published in Italy as *I Love You* (Milano: Cooperativa Libraria I.U.L.M., 1996).

19. The translation in the Jerusalem Bible is "the most subtle of all the wild beasts." I have deliberately substituted the word "creature." As Paul ricoeur reminds us (*Symbolism of Evil,* 259), in the Jewish tradition the rabbis always made a point of remembering that the serpent, too, was one of God's creatures.

20. Eisenberg and Abécassis, *Bible ouverte,* 218.

21. Ibid.

22. [It is perhaps worth noting that in the French of *La Bible de Jérusalem,* the word translated as "pleasing" to the eye in English is *séduisant,* "seductive," a meaning even more germane to the author's point. —Trans.]

23. I am describing succinctly here the transition from an instinctive animal attitude to a religious one, that is, from animality to the sacred. René Girard has worked out very convincingly how the victimizing mechanism works, how the violence of all suddenly becomes polarized against an individual who comes to be viewed simultaneously as the one responsible for disorder and as the restorer of order. All the gods, Girard concludes, began as scapegoats. That sort of idolatrous passion, hateful adoration of the model who becomes the obstacle to the accomplishment of my desire, bears witness on the individual level to the genesis of the sacred in the bosom of mimetic conflict.

24. [The French word that appears three times in this paragraph and frequently in other parts of the text that I translate as "self-misunderstanding," "failure to understand properly," or more frequently simply as "misunderstanding" is *méconnaissance,* literally "mis-knowing"; it is frequently used by Girard and by other French writers on psychology, especially Jacques Lacan (in whose English translations it is usually left untranslated), to refer to a kind of willful ignorance and misinterpretation of one's own motives, a refusal of self-recognition. —Trans.]

25. [The French original of the *Bible de Jérusalem* is slightly different in meaning here in a way that is significant for the author's interpretation. The English translation of God's question is: "Who told you that you were naked?" The French is "Et qui t'a appris que tu étais nu?" "Qui t'a appris?" also carries the connotations "Who led you to know?" or "Who made you aware [of it]?" The underlining in this quotation and in the next iterations of it are the author's. —Trans.]

26. Cf. the interpretation of the *skandalon* in René Girard, *Things Hidden since the Foundation of the World* (Stanford, CA: Stanford University Press, 1987), and *Les origines de la culture: Entretiens avec Pierpaolo Antonello et João Cezar de Castro Rocha* (Pluriel. Paris: Hachette, 2006). See also René Girard, with Pierpaolo Antonello and João Cezar de Castro Rocha, *Evolution and Conversion* (London: Continuum International Publishing, 2007). [The term "*skandalon*" is used in the New Testament to refer to Jesus as a "stumbling block" for those in the cultures of his time who expected some other sort of messianic leader (I Cor. 1:23; Rom. 11:9). For René Girard, it also refers to Jesus's role as a scapegoat. —Trans.]

27. [In the *Bible de Jérusalem:* "m'a donné de l'arbre." —Trans.]

28. Eisenberg and Abécassis, *Bible ouverte,* 329–30.

29. Ricoeur, *Symbolism of Evil,* 251.

30. Ibid.

31. [The word translated into English as "yearning" from the *Bible de Jérusalem* is *"convoitise"* in the French ("Ta *convoitise* te poussera vers ton mari . . ."), a word defined in the *Dictionnaire Robert* as "an extreme and unscrupulous desire for possession." "Covetousness" connotes that meaning more precisely in English than "yearning" (which normally suggests desire that is strong but not necessarily unscrupulous or even violent). I have translated this word as "covetousness" in other parts of the text where the author has used it. —Trans.]

32. [Here I am departing from the English of the *New Jerusalem Bible,* which translates it as "he must not be allowed to reach out his hand and pick from the tree of life." In the French of

the *Bible de Jérusalem,* this is "Qu'il n'étende la main ...": not *"He must not be allowed to reach out his hand ..."* but *"Let him not. ..."* —a meaning that fits better with Oughourlian's suggestion that God does not so much prohibit as warn and does not so much punish as point out consequences. —Trans.]

33. René Girard, *Things Hidden since the Foundation of the World,* Research Undertaken in Collaboration with Jean-Michel Oughourlian and Guy Lefort, trans. Stephen Bann and Michael Metteer (Stanford, CA: Stanford University Press, 1987), 33.

CHAPTER THREE. UNIVERSAL MIMESIS

1. Scheler, *The Nature of Sympathy,* trans. Peter Heath (New Haven: Yale University Press, 1954), 213. Italics in original.

2. Ibid., 215.

3. Ibid., 108. Italics in original.

4. Arthur Schopenhauer, *The World as Will and Representation* (New York: Dover Publications, 1966).

5. Henri Bergson, *Creative Evolution* (Cosimo Classics: New York, 2005), 206.

6. Ibid., 210.

7. Pierre Montebello, *L'autre métaphysique: essai sur la philosophie de la nature: Ravaisson, Tarde, Nietzsche et Bergson* (Paris: Desclée de Brouwer, 2003), 10.

8. Ibid., 11.

9. Ibid., 12.

10. Stanford University Press, 1991. See especially pages 189–95.

11. Franz Anton Mesmer, *Dissertatio physico-medica de planetarum inflexu* (A Physical-Medical Dissertation on the Curving of the Planets), in Franz Anton Mesmer and Robert Amadou, *Le Magnétisme animal. Oeuvres publiées* (Paris: Payot, 1971), 33–34.

12. Elias Canetti, *Crowds and Power,* trans. Carol Stewart (New York: Farrar, Strauss and Giroux, 1984), 16.

13. Ibid.

14. Gustave Le Bon, *The Crowd* (New Brunswick, NJ: Transaction Publishers, 1995), 47.

15. Wystan Hugh Auden, "Nones," in *The Shield of Achilles* (New York: Random House, 1955), 73–74.

16. *Des choses cachées depuis la fondation du monde* (Paris: Grasset, 1978), translated as *Things Hidden since the Foundation of the World* (Palo Alto, CA: Stanford University Press, 1987).

17. Giacomo Rizzolati, Leonardo Fogassi, and Vittorio Gallese, "Les neurones miroirs," *Pour la science* 351 (Jan. 2007): 44.

18. Vittorio Gallese, "The Intentional Attunement Hypothesis: The Mirror Neuron System and Its Role in Interpersonal Relations," in International AI-Workshop on NeuroBotics, Stefan Wermter, Günther Palm, and Mark Elshaw, *Biomimetic Neural Learning for Intelligent Robots:*

Intelligent Systems, Cognitive Robotics, and Neuroscience (Berlin: Springer, 2005), 19–30. The text is also accessible online at http://www.interdisciplines.org/mirror/papers/1.

19. Andrew Meltzoff and Jean Decety, "What Imitation Tells Us about Social Cognition: A Rapprochement between Developmental Psychology and Cognitive Neuroscience," *Philosophical Transactions of the Royal Society: Biological Sciences* 358 (2003): 496.

20. Ibid.

21. Colwyn Trevarthen, T. Kokkinaki, and Geraldo Fiamenghi, "What Infants' Imitations Communicate: With Mothers, with Fathers, with Peers," in Jacqueline Nadel and George Butterworth, eds., *Imitation in Infancy* (Cambridge: Cambridge University Press, 1999), 127–85.

22. *Le Figaro,* interview of 5 February 2005.

23. Rizzolati, Fogassi, and Gallese, "Les neurones miroirs," *Pour la science* 351 (Jan. 2007). My emphasis.

24. Gallese, "The Intentional Attunement Hypothesis: The Mirror Neuron System and Its Role in Interpersonal Relations," accessible online at http://www.interdisciplines.org/mirror/papers/1.

25. Rizzolati, Fogassi, and Gallese, "Les neurones miroirs," *Pour la science* 351 (Jan. 2007): 53.

26. 44–46.

27. For a more detailed discussion, see my *Puppet of Desire,* ch. 6, especially 206–26.

28. Léon Chertok, *Sense and Nonsense in Psychotherapy: The Challenge of Hypnosis,* trans. R. H. Ahrenfeldt and revised by the author (Oxford: Pergamon Press, 1981), 178.

29. See, for example, Girard's *Deceit, Desire, and the Novel,* ch. 11, and *To Double Business Bound.*

30. Elaine Nicpon Marieb, *Human Anatomy and Physiology* (San Francisco: Pearson/Benjamin Cummings, 2004), 455.

Chapter Four. The Clinical Analysis of Rivalry

1. Oughourlian, *Puppet of Desire,* 128–30, 141–42, drawing on Michel Leiris, *La possession et ses aspects théâtraux chez les Éthiopiens de Gondar, précédé de La croyance aux génies zâr en Éthiopie du Nord.* I will discuss this example of benign possession further below.

2. Oughourlian, *Puppet of Desire,* 184–85.

3. Pierre Briquet, *Traité clinique et thérapeutique de l'hystérie,* 374. My emphasis. This text takes on a particular interest in light of what we now know about mirror neurons.

4. See Girard, Oughourlian, and Lefort, *Things Hidden since the Foundation of the World,* book 3, "Interdividual Psychology."

5. Oughourlian, *Puppet of Desire,* ch. 3, "Possession: Exorcism," and ch. 4, "Possession: Adorcism."

6. Leiris, *La Croyance aux génies zâr en Ethiopie du Nord,* 25–26.

7. Ibid., 85.

8. See Oughourlian, *Puppet of Desire,* ch. 5, "Hysteria."

Epilogue. Can One Rescue a Relationship?

1. Saadi, *Le Jardin des roses* (Paris: Albin Michel, 1962), 228.

2. André Breton, *Mad Love,* trans. Mary Ann Caws (Lincoln: University of Nebraska Press, 1987), 99.

3. D. H. Lawrence, *The Plumed Serpent* (Hertfordshire, UK: Wordsworth Classics, 1995), 228.

Selected Bibliography

Anspach, Mark Rogin. *A charge de revanche: figures élémentaires de la réciprocité. La couleur des idées.* Paris: Seuil, 2002. Bataille, Georges. *L'Alleluiah.* Paris: Gallimard, coll. "L'Imaginaire," 1998.

Bergson, Henri. *Creative Evolution.* New York: Cosimo Classics, 2005.

Blackmore, Susan. *La Théorie des mèmes, pourquoi nous nous imitons les uns les autres.* Max Milo, 2006.

Breton, André. *Mad Love = L'Amour Fou.* Lincoln: University of Nebraska Press, 1987.

Briquet, Pierre. *Traité clinique et thérapeutique de l'hystérie.* Paris: J.-B. Baillière et fils, 1859.

Canetti, Elias. *Crowds and Power.* Translated by Carol Stewart. New York: Farrar, Strauss and Giroux, 1984.

Chertok, Léon. *Sense and Nonsense in Psychotherapy: The Challenge of Hypnosis.* Translated by R. H. Ahrenfeldt and revised by the author. Oxford: Pergamon Press, 1981.

Chouraqui, André. *La Bible.* Paris: Desclee De Brouwer, 1974.

Cyrulnik, Boris. *Un merveilleux malheur.* Paris: Odile Jacob, 1999; Poches O. Jacob, 2002.

Eisenberg, Josy, and Armand Abécassis. *A Bible ouverte.* II, *Et Dieu créa Éve.* "Présences du judaisme." Paris: Albin Michel, 1979.

Freedberg, David, and Vittorio Gallese. "Motion, Emotion and Empathy in Esthetic Experience." *Trends in Cognitive Sciences* 11, no. 5 (2007): 197.

Freud, Sigmund. *Group Psychology and the Analysis of the Ego.* The International Psycho-analytical Library, no. 6. London, Vienna: International Psychoanalytical Press, 1922.

Gallese, Vittorio. "Embodied Simulation: From Neurons to Phenomenal Experience." *Phenomenology and the Cognitive Sciences* 4, no. 1 (2005): 23–48.

Gallese, Vittorio. "The Intentional Attunement Hypothesis: The Mirror Neuron System and Its Role in Interpersonal Relations." In International AI-Workshop on NeuroBotics, Stefan

Wermter, Günther Palm, and Mark Elshaw, *Biomimetic Neural Learning for Intelligent Robots: Intelligent Systems, Cognitive Robotics, and Neuroscience,* 19–30. Berlin: Springer, 2005. (Also accessible online at http://www.interdisciplines.org/mirror/papers/1.)

Gallese, Vittorio. "Intentional Attunement: A Neurophysiological Perspective on Social Cognition and Its Disruption in Autism." *Brain Research* 1079 (2006): 15. (Also accessible online at http://www.interdisciplines.org/mirror/papers/1.)

Gallese, Vittorio. "The Manifold Nature of Interpersonal Relations: The Quest for a Common Mechanism." *Philosophical Transactions: Biological Sciences* 358, no. 1431 (2003): 517–528.

Gallese, Vittorio. "The Roots of Empathy: The Shared Manifold Hypothesis and the Neural Basis of Intersubjectivity." *Psychopathology* 36, no. 4 (2003): 171–80.

Gallese, Vittorio. "The Shared Manifold Hypothesis: From Neurons to Empathy." *Journal of Consciousness Studies* 85, no. 5–7 (2001): 33–50.

Garrels, Scott R. "Imitation, Mirror Neurons, and Mimetic Desire." *Contagion* 12–13 (2006): 47–86.

Girard, René. *Deceit, Desire, and the Novel: Self and Other in Literary Structure.* Translated by Yvonne Freccero. Baltimore: Johns Hopkins University Press, 1965.

Girard, René. *Violence and the Sacred.* Translated by Patrick Gregory. Baltimore: Johns Hopkins University Press, 1977.

Girard, René. *"To Double Business Bound": Essays on Literature, Mimesis, and Anthropology.* Baltimore: Johns Hopkins University Press, 1978.

Girard, René, Jean-Michel Oughourlian, and Guy Lefort. *Things Hidden since the Foundation of the World.* Translated by Stephen Bann and Michael Metteer. Stanford, CA: Stanford University Press, 1987.

Girard, René, João Cezar de Castro Rocha, and Pierpaolo Antonello. *Evolution and Conversion: Dialogues on the Origins of Culture.* London: T & T Clark, 2007.

Guillaume, Paul. *L'Imitation chez l'enfant.* Paris: Felix Alcan, 1926.

Keukelaere, Simon de. "Des découvertes révolutionnaires en sciences cognitives—les paradoxes et dangers de l'imitation." *Automates intelligents,* no. 63 (2005).

Keukelaere, Simon de. "La Violence humaine: imitation ou memes? Critique d'un point de vue girardien." *Automates intelligents* (2002).

Lawrence, D. H. *The Plumed Serpent.* Hertfordshire, UK: Wordsworth Classics, 1995.

Le Bon, Gustave. *The Crowd.* New Brunswick, N.J.: Transaction, 1995.

Marieb, Elaine Nicpon. *Human Anatomy & Physiology,* 6th ed. San Francisco: Pearson/Benjamin Cummings, 2004.

Leiris, Michel. *La possession et ses aspects théâtraux chez les Éthiopiens de Gondar, précédé de La croyance aux génies zâr en Éthiopie du Nord.* Les Hommes et leurs signes. Paris: Le Sycomore, 1980.

Meltzoff, Andrew N., and Jean Decety. "What Imitation Tells Us about Social Cognition: A Rapprochement between Developmental Psychology and Cognitive Neuroscience." *Philosophical Transactions of the Royal Society: Biological Sciences* 358 (2003): 491–500.

Meltzoff, Andrew N., and Wolfgang Prinz. *The Imitative Mind: Development, Evolution, and Brain Bases.* Cambridge Studies in Cognitive Perceptual Development. Cambridge, U.K.: Cambridge University Press, 2002.

Mesmer, Franz Anton, and Robert Amadou. *Le Magnétisme animal. Oeuvres publiées.* Paris: Payot, 1971.

Montebello, Pierre. *L'autre métaphysique: essai sur la philosophie de la nature: Ravaisson, Tarde, Nietzsche et Bergson.* Paris: Desclée de Brouwer, 2003.

Newton, Isaac. *Philosophia naturalis principia mathematica.* London: Wm. Dawson, 1953.

Nietzsche, Friedrich Wilhelm, translated by Walter Arnold Kaufmann. *The Gay Science; With a Prelude in Rhymes and an Appendix of Songs.* New York: Vintage Books, 1974.

Oughourlian, Jean-Michel. *The Puppet of Desire: The Psychology of Hysteria, Possession, and Hypnosis.* Translated with an introduction by Eugene Webb. Stanford, CA: Stanford University Press, 1991.

Ramachandran, Vilayanur. *A Brief Tour of Human Consciousness: From Impostor Poodles to Purple Numbers.* Pi Press (Pearson Education), 2004.

Ramachandran, Vilayanur. "Mirror Neurons and Imitation Learning as the Driving Force behind 'the Great Leap Forward' in Human Evolution." *Edge* 69 (June 1, 2000). (Also accessible online at http://www.edge.org/documents/archive/edge69.html.)

Ricœur, Paul. *The Symbolism of Evil.* Translated by Emerson Buchanan. Boston: Beacon Press, 1969.

Rizzolati, Giacomo. *Les Neurones miroirs.* Paris: Odile Jacob, 2007.

Rizzolati, Giacomo, and M. A. Arbib. "Language within Our Grasp." *Trends in Neurosciences* 21 (1998): 188–194.

Rizzolati, Giacomo, and Laila Craighero. "The Mirror Neuron System." *Annual Review of Neuroscience* 27 (2004): 169–192.

Rizzolati, Giacomo, Leonardo Fogassi, and Vittorio Gallese. "Les neurones miroirs." *Pour la science* 351 (Jan. 2007): 44–49.

Rizzolati, Giacomo, Leonardo Fogassi, and Vittorio Gallese. "Neurophysiological Mechanisms Underlying the Understanding and Imitation of Action." *Nature Reviews Neuroscience* 2 (2001): 661–670.

Rizzolati, Giacomo, M. A. Umiltà, E. Kohler, V. Gallese, L. Fogassi, L. Fadiga, and C. Keysers. "I Know What You Are Doing: A Neurophysiological Study." *Neuron* 31 (July 2001): 155–165.

Scheler, Max. *The Nature of Sympathy.* Translated by Peter Heath. New Haven: Yale University Press, 1954.

Schopenhauer, Arthur. *The World as Will and Representation.* New York: Dover Publications, 1966.

Tarde, Gabriel. *Oeuvres de Gabriel Tarde,* vol. 1, *Monadologie et Sociologie,* Collection "Les Empecheurs de penser en rond," Institut Synthélabo pour le progrès de la connaissance, Le Plessis-Robinson, 1999.

Thouret, Michel-Augustin. *Extrait de la correspondance de la Société royale de médecine relativement au magnétisme animal.* Paris: l'Imprimérie royale, 1785.

Trevarthen, Colwyn, T. Kokkinaki, and Geraldo Fiamenghi. "What Infants' Imitations Communicate: With Mothers, with Fathers, with Peers." In *Imitation in Infancy,* edited by J. Nadel and G. Butterworth, 127–85. Cambridge: Cambridge University Press, 1999.

Webb, Eugene. *The Self Between: From Freud to the New Social Psychology of France.* Seattle: University of Washington Press, 1993.

Index